Start Your Own

COIN-OPERATED
LAUNDRY

Additional titles in *Entrepreneur's* **Startup Series**

Start Your Own

Entrepreneur MAGAZINE'S

startup

2ND EDITION

Start Your Own

COIN-OPERATED LAUNDRY

Your Step-by-Step Guide to Success

Entrepreneur Press and Mandy Erickson

Ep
Entrepreneur
Press

Editorial Director: Jere L. Calmes
Managing Editor: Marla Markman
Cover Design: Beth Hansen-Winter
Production: Eliot House Productions
Composition: Patricia Miller

This publication is designed to provide accurate and authoritative information in regard to the subject matter covered. It is sold with the understanding that the publisher is not engaged in rendering legal, accounting or other professional services. If legal advice or other expert assistance is required, the services of a competent professional person should be sought.

Library of Congress Cataloging-in-Publication Data
Erickson, Mandy.
    Start your own coin-operated laundry/by Entrepreneur Press and Mandy Erickson.— 2nd. ed.
      p.   cm.
    ISBN 1-59918-028-6 (alk. paper)
      1. Laundry industry—Management. 2. Self-service laundries—Management. 3. New business enterprises—Management. I. Entrepreneur Press. II. Title.
    HD9999.L382E75 2006
    648'.10681—dc22   2006013264

Printed in Canada

12 11 10 09 08 07 06   10 9 8 7 6 5 4 3 2 1

Contents

▲

Preface

When I was working on this book, several people told me that they had considered opening a self-service laundry. "It seems like such an easy business," they said. "You just set out the machines and people drop money into them."

If you open a laundry with that attitude, I chided them, you can be sure your business will fail.

Running a laundry is like owning a café—customers will spend a good chunk of their days in your store, and they want to feel comfortable. If you or your staff welcome them, answer their questions cheerfully, listen to their life stories, they'll come back. When you decorate the store, keep it clean and the machines in working order, so that customers will bring their clothes to your laundry rather than the dingy place around the corner.

In short, the more effort you put into your laundry business, the more you'll get out of it, financially and personally. And that's where this book comes in: It'll help you get the most from your venture.

Perhaps most importantly, you'll learn how to research a location to see whether your business will sink or swim. You'll need to know, for example, whether the people who live near the store are likely to use laundries, or if most of them have washers in their homes. You'll discover when it's best to buy an existing laundry and when it makes more sense to build a new one. And you'll learn how to determine the value of a laundry for sale.

When you've found a location, this book will help you find the right equipment. You'll learn what the correct ratio of washers to dryers is and how to configure the machines so your customers can clean their clothes quickly and easily. This book will also give you some pointers for decorating your store in a way that draws customers. It includes ideas for extra services, such as a snack bar, Internet access, or a play area for kids.

In addition, you'll discover the pros and cons of staffing a laundry. While attendants keep the store clean and help customers, their salaries add more costs, and supervising adds headaches. Should you decide to hire attendants, this book will give you pointers on finding employees and keeping them motivated.

This book will also help you attract new customers to your store through advertisements and promotions. You'll hear from seasoned laundry owners about the marketing tactics that worked for them—and you'll save money by avoiding those that didn't.

Finally, you'll learn how to keep track of your finances so you can squeeze as much profit as possible out of your business. You'll know how to price your machines so you're competitive but still earning a buck, and you'll find out whether your employees justify their cost. You'll also get some tips on tax deductions specific to laundries.

As comprehensive as this book is, it can't tell you everything you need to know to start up a self-service laundry. A lot depends on your finances, your city and state, the competition in your area, the clientele, and your equipment. So I've included an appendix full of resources—including consultants, suppliers, associations, magazines, and manuals—to help you find answers to your questions.

Starting up a laundry business is a big commitment, emotionally and financially. You want to weigh your decisions as carefully as possible, consider all the options and be aware of potential downfalls. This book will help you do that.

1

The New
Laundromat

The coin-operated laundry industry has undergone a revolution. No longer dingy, unsafe, boring places that customers must endure on a weekly basis, laundromats are becoming fun and attractive multiservice centers that customers enjoy visiting. "The industry is now getting a facelift," says Brian Wallace, president and CEO of the Coin Laundry

Association, a national association for self-service laundry owners. "There's a trend toward coin laundries being more comfortable for the customer."

The newer laundries have snack bars, a place to drop off and pick up dry cleaning, and video games. Some of them don't even use coins. Instead, customers use swipe cards that subtract the cost of the wash or dry, much like a phone card or debit card. Many laundry owners also employ attendants to keep an eye on the store and help customers use the equipment.

If you're thinking about getting into the self-service laundry business, the first thing you need to have is a clear picture of the industry—where it has been and where it's likely to go. In this chapter, we'll take a look back at the history of laundromats, and we'll discuss current industry trends as well as the market outlook. In short, we'll give you the skinny on what you need to know before launching your own laundry business.

Laundromat Renaissance

The coin-operated laundry industry is changing in response to several trends currently impacting the business. The first is that, for most of us, meeting the demands of work and our personal lives leads to a time crunch—there just aren't enough hours in the day to accomplish everything we would like to. Laundry owners are capitalizing on this reality by offering their customers time-saving convenience in the form of wash-and-fold (drop-off service) and dry-cleaning service. Some are even picking up laundry from customers' homes and delivering it back to them clean and folded.

In addition, owners have realized that they can maximize their profits by providing customers with access to multiple services. Since they're paying a set amount of rent on their commercial spaces, they might as well use those spaces to its fullest potential. Many owners around the country are serving food, renting mailboxes, and offering free internet access. Because the new laundries are bigger than in the past—often 3,000 or 4,000 square feet—overhead is higher, and owners are looking for ways to cover the cost. These additional services demand little increase in overhead because the rent is already paid. Customers benefit by being able to use several services all in one convenient location.

Cindy Patel, who has owned Mountain Wash Laundry in Shelby, North Carolina, for a

Bright Idea

If you have a friend who's a manicurist, a palm reader, a masseur, or something else that could complement your business, ask if he or she wants to offer those services in your laundry. Your friend will benefit from the captive audience, and you may draw more business from people who want to get their nails done and their clothes washed at the same time.

year, says that she is opening a snack bar and a minimart in her laundry. "I have a big space, 6,000 square feet," she says, "and this will help pay for it."

Paul Partyka, editor of *American Coin-Op*, a magazine devoted to self-service laundries, says that Patel's approach is the norm these days. "Trying to generate additional revenue per square foot has always been an issue," he says. "But it's even more so now with tighter competition and utility bills growing. Everybody wants to squeeze as much money as possible out of their spaces. Looking for an extra service that will work is always on their minds."

Another trend laundry owners have recognized is that customers prefer to visit laundromats with more pleasant atmospheres. Many laundry owners are building kids' centers, holding music concerts, giving away coffee, and hiring attendants who are friendly and helpful. "I don't think we'll ever cross that threshold into making laundry fun," Wallace says, "but we're making it more comfortable."

Tom Leavitt, owner of Darcies Laundry in the Seattle area, opened three new stores, all of them near older, smaller laundries, most of which have since closed. Darcies offers customers a better deal: bigger stores with play areas for children and attendants on duty at all times. "Our stores are very convenient," Leavitt says. "They're clean, they have a friendly environment, and they have a lot of machines, so you can get in and out of there as fast as possible."

The Good News

As the population of the United States grows, the number of renters—your main market—is likely to grow, too. Other social phenomena, like the prevalence of two-income families, suggest that convenient services such as wash-and-fold will continue to grow in popularity as working parents have less time to attend to household chores like laundry.

According to a survey from the Coin Laundry Association, more than half of coin laundries offer wash-and-fold. "It's by far the number-one extra service for laundries," says Partyka. "It's doing well." Partyka also notes that even people with washers and dryers at home are using self-service laundries for the sake of convenience. With the regular capacity machines used in homes, it can take quite a lot of time to do load after load—and that's where laundromats come in. "They just run over to the coin laundry, use a couple of the large machines and knock it off," he says. In other words, although the majority of laundromat customers are low- to middle-income renters, some laundries are tapping into higher-income markets by offering convenience: wash-and-fold service and large machines.

In addition, office dress codes are growing increasingly less formal. And as more people wear casual clothing (which doesn't require dry cleaning) to work and leave the nicer duds for special occasions, you may find that consumers will be making more trips to the laundromat.

The Bad News

While the trends we've mentioned are favorable for entrepreneurs entering the laundry business, they don't suggest that business is booming. The industry is what experts describe as a "mature market." Save for areas that are seeing high population growth, pretty much every neighborhood that needs a laundry has one—or two or three that are competing vigorously. In some areas of the country, there are already too many laundromats.

However, there is room for new laundry owners. Many get into the business by purchasing an existing laundry and renovating it. Some also find that they can build a new laundry in an area with competing laundries and thrive by offering a bigger store, more services and better customer relations. Another way to get into the business is to locate your store where there is the best potential need for a new laundry: in an area that's experiencing population growth.

So as you consider getting into the laundry business, keep the words "mature market" in mind. Don't buy a store just because it's for sale or build a store just because you have a great idea for a new gimmick. You'll need to be very careful to make sure there's enough of a customer base to make your business thrive. You may be able to draw a little extra business from people who like using your store better because of its cleanliness

Dollars and Cents

Accoording to *American Coin-Op* magazine, these are some typical prices that laundry owners charge for using the following equipment or services:

- ○ Top-load washer: $1.50 per load
- ○ 18-pound front-load washer: $1.75 per load
- ○ 20-pound front-load washer: $2.00 per load
- ○ 35-pound front-load washer: $3.50 per load
- ○ Dryer: $0.25 per 10 minutes
- ○ Wash-and-fold: $0.90 per pound
- ○ Vended detergent: $0.50 per box

or from people who use your wash-and-fold service, but the core of your business will be people who just want to get their laundry done quickly and conveniently. If there are already enough laundromats in the neighborhood to serve their needs, they're not as likely to patronize your store.

Finally, you also need to consider that getting into the laundry business requires a large initial investment. The average-size laundromat will cost you in the neighborhood of $200,000 to $500,000—whether you choose to purchase an existing laundry or build one in a retail space.

The Annals of Laundromats

Let's step back for a minute to see how the self-service laundry industry got to where it is today. It all started with the first wringer washer, built in 1907. During the Depression, enterprising businesspeople started using wringer washers to operate public laundries. These businesses were originally drop-off services, where customers left their laundry to have someone wash it for them.

Later on, customers could rent the machines to use themselves. "People took wringer washers and put them into buildings," says Lionel Bogut, a laundry expert who has been in the business for more than 50 years. "They would tap hot water to each of the washers, and people would come in and rent them for an hour or two."

Electric washers were not produced until the late 1930s. When manufacturers eventually added coin slots to the machines in the late 1950s, true coin-operated laundries came into existence. A coin-laundry construction boom followed. There was such a high demand for these stores that anyone who built one was almost guaranteed a profit. The owners of coin-operated laundries didn't need to keep their stores clean and machines working to attract customers and make a profit. As a result, many laundromats were kept in poor condition.

The industry deteriorated as broken machines stayed broken, stores were left dirty, and vandals and thieves took advantage of the lack of owners' attention. In the 1960s, however, the industry experienced a resurgence. Smart new investors realized they could do better than run-down, unattended stores and started creating spiffy new businesses. They built larger stores, hired attendants, and added dry cleaning and clothing repair.

This revitalization didn't last long, though. During the oil crisis of the 1970s, the industry saw another downturn as energy costs cut into profits and rising interest rates scared off new investors. But the industry recovered in the 1980s, due in large part to the production of new, energy-efficient equipment by manufacturers. Since that time, the number of laundromats has steadily grown; today there are approximately 35,000 laundromats countrywide.

▲

The Laundromat Life

If you're planning on operating just one or two stores, you'll be in good company. Three-quarters of laundry owners own only one store, and very few have more than two. While there are no national laundry chains, a few local chains are starting to grow in various parts of the country. These chains are still quite localized, though, and only a few consist of more than a few dozen.

For a little more than half of laundry owners, operating the store(s) is their full-time job. Others take the moonlighting approach—they manage other businesses or work a day job. But more laundry owners are starting to own larger stores and more than one store. These people are able to survive on the income larger stores or multiple stores generate.

The amount of money you can make from a laundry varies tremendously. According to the Coin Laundry Association's Brian Wallace, the annual gross income from one store can range from $30,000 to $1 million. The expenses incurred while running a store range between 65 and 115 percent of the gross income. That means that a store grossing $30,000 per year, at best nets $10,500 and at worst loses $4,500. For a store grossing $1 million per year, the profit could be as high as $350,000, or there could be a loss of up to $150,000, depending on expenses.

Wallace says these profit margins have less to do with the size of the store than with its owner. An owner who runs his or her store well—who keeps it clean, repairs its

Businesses Have Laundry, Too

A laundry can service more than families washing clothes and sheets. If you offer wash-and-fold, consider approaching small businesses that might need laundry done on a regular basis: hair salons, pet groomers, day spas, motels, caterers, schools, and restaurants.

Before you start knocking on doors, however, be sure you have your wash-and-fold system well-greased. And you'll need some wheels: Commercial customers will likely want you to pick up and deliver the laundry, as they're busy running their own enterprises. They may also expect you to invoice them, so you'll need to be ready to send out monthly bills.

Tom Leavitt of Darcies Laundry in Seattle has been successful with his commercial route. "There is a niche in the market for those who need laundry services who can't afford the really big commercial laundries," he says. But he cautions that the commercial accounts take some work to build and maintain: "It takes someone out there selling constantly."

Stat Fact

According to *American Coin-Op* magazine, the top expenses for laundry owners include utilities, rent, employees, insurance, maintenance and parts, and loan payments.

equipment quickly, uses energy-efficient systems and offers good customer service—will see profit margins of about 35 percent.

The steady income that a laundry generates is a plus for many people. If you're looking for a business that will keep the cash flowing no matter what the rest of the economy is doing, you've found it in laundries. Clean clothes are a necessity, not a luxury, so people are going to use laundromats no matter how the stock market is performing. The business is also fairly steady month in, month out. So unless you draw on vacationers' dollars in a place with seasonal tourism, you'll find that you can count on a fairly steady income throughout the year.

But remember, the laundry business is not growing; it's mature. There are about as many stores as there is dirty laundry to fill them. To ensure your business will survive, you'll need to make sure your laundromat is in a location that's convenient for people who use laundromats. And to make your business thrive, you'll need to give your customers something they don't get in other laundromats—a nice atmosphere, good customer service, and entertainment.

By now, you should have a much clearer picture of what the industry looks like. The next thing you'll need to think about is whether the laundry business is the right fit for you. In Chapter 2, we'll delve into what it's really like to own a laundry store, and we'll give you an idea of the personality traits that are best suited to this kind of business.

Is It
for You?

Now that you know the history of the laundry business and where it's headed, you'll need to think about whether running a laundromat is the right business opportunity for you. Does it suit your personality? Do you know what a typical "day in the life" is like? This chapter is designed to help you tackle these questions and see if the laundry business is a good fit.

No Experience Necessary

None of the entrepreneurs interviewed for this book had experience in the laundry business when they first started out. One had a resume that included milking cows, another was a contractor, yet another ran a rental equipment business. Most just decided that starting a laundry was a good business opportunity. However, they all recommend that new entrepreneurs research the business by talking to laundry owners, joining associations, and reading the trade literature.

Tom Leavitt, who opened three stores in the Seattle area with a partner, put some time into planning the laundries. "We traveled around the country, looked at a lot of other operations, and designed our prototype," he says. "We took care to figure out what would work the best." He and his partner also attended a Coin Laundry Association convention in Chicago and took a tour of laundries in the area.

Collette Clarkson knew nothing about the business before she started a laundromat in Evans, Colorado, with Kim Clarkson, her business partner. But the two got to work when Collette's uncle, who was building a strip mall, asked if she'd be interested in operating a laundromat. "We did a lot of research," Collette says. They spoke to a number of laundry owners about the business and read as many issues of trade magazines as they could find.

"Be patient and do your homework," advises Brian Wallace, president and CEO of the Coin Laundry Association. "You'd be absolutely amazed how quickly someone will get into business and spend their life savings without doing any research whatsoever."

While no particular experience is necessary, a business background is always important. In addition, a background in machine repair or a knack for fixing machines helps. Owners who have experience with laundry equipment are able to cut down on the cost of repairs. But others have found that they can learn about the machines and make some repairs themselves, or hire a repairperson and avoid the headache altogether. The self-service laundry business is an open club. With enough enthusiasm, interest, and business-savvy, you can join the club and succeed in the industry.

The Laundromat Personality

You may think that the laundry business is about clothes, but what it's really about is people. It's a service business, and like any service business, you need to treat your customers well if you want them to return to your store.

If you're friendly, your customers will want to use your store. By taking the time to talk to them, you will also be able to learn about their laundry needs and their preferences for services. Ultimately, this kind of information will help you improve the

Beware!
When you talk with other laundry owners to learn about their experiences with the business, avoid your own neighborhood. Your competitors will be reluctant to help you out, and you don't want someone giving bad advice in the hope that your business will fail.

quality of your business so that you can attract even more customers.

Even if you decide to hire employees and leave the customer relations to them, you still need good people skills to hire and supervise employees. The more closely you work with them and the better they know and like you, the better job they'll do.

If you have an unattended laundry that you visit twice a day to clean and collect quarters, you still need to greet your customers with a smile on your face and an attitude that's ready to help. So if small talk with strangers leaves you cold, and you can't stand the thought of answering customers' questions (often the same ones over and over), the laundry business may not be the one for you.

However, if you think you'll like meeting new people, helping them work the machines, and listening to them talk while they wait for the dryers to finish, you'll find this business rewarding. "Interacting with customers—that's the best part," says Collette Clarkson. "I can't even imagine how many regulars we have who we know by name."

Suit Your Style

The good news about owning a laundry is that you can shape your business to fit your own tastes. You can hire employees, offer a variety of fabric care services and run a full-fledged operation; or you can keep things simple by opening a small, unattended laundry. The other piece of good news is that you don't need a background in running laundromats or taking care of laundry equipment, though you do need to research the business.

The bad news is that you need lots of money up front to buy an existing laundry or to build one in a leased space ($200,000 to $500,000 on average). And while you can earn money from a laundry while you work elsewhere, you still need to keep the store in good working order by supervising employees, fixing machines and collecting the money.

Bright Idea
If you're not sure you'll like the laundry business, try working in a laundromat for a while. Volunteer at a nearby store or take a temporary job. You'll have a much better idea of whether the business is for you after working in a laundry, even after only a few days.

Self-Help

The beauty of owning a self-service laundry is that your customers help themselves. You

▲

Top Headaches

Every year *American Coin-Op* magazine conducts a survey of its readers to find out what the top problems are for laundromat owners. The list varies little, says Paul Partyka, editor of the magazine. "The order may change, but the issues are the same every year," he says. So if you're like most other laundromat owners, you can expect to face the following challenges in running your business:

○ High cost of utilities

○ Dealing with employees

○ Competition

○ High cost of doing business

○ High rent

○ Vandalism

○ Maintenance

don't have to be at your store; you don't even have to hire someone to be at your store. You can work at another job or run another business while your customers are dropping coin after coin into your machines. For entrepreneurs who don't want the hassle of hiring employees and writing paychecks, this is a big incentive.

"I like the fact that it's pretty stress-free," says Brian De Coster, who owns four unattended laundries in and around Iowa City, Iowa. "The laundry business is really a breath of fresh air." De Coster's other job is running an equipment rental business, so he's always worried about having enough employees and equipment to respond to customers' demands. His laundromats, on the other hand, require only a quick visit twice a day to clean and collect money. He rarely has an emergency, except when a machine breaks and he needs to call a repairperson or make an extra visit to fix it.

While the laundry business can be fairly stress free, it can also interest entrepreneurs who want to take more active roles. Owners who hire attendants and offer wash-and-fold service have much more work to do, but they also reap greater financial—and personal—rewards.

"We've worked really hard, and we're really proud of the business," Collette Clarkson says. "We just try to provide really good service."

Caring for Your Store

The laundry business might appeal to you because you don't have to work at it eight hours per day like other jobs. It's true—you can set out your machines and let them collect money while you do something else. But don't get carried away with the idea. Even if you don't have attendants to supervise, you need to make sure your store is sparkling clean, equipment is working properly, the change machines are full, and your books are in order.

"It's a pretty simple business," says Tim O'Connell, who owns 24 Colonial Laundromat stores in the Syracuse, New York, area. But he stresses that the stores need to remain clean at all times: "Nothing grosses people out more than dirt. We keep them immaculately clean and brightly lit, provide a safe environment, and keep the machines running properly."

And if you do hire attendants, they must be supervised closely. Most attendants make minimum wage or slightly more, so you can't expect them to take too active an interest in the success of your business. You must visit the store enough to be sure that it's running properly and employees are productive. For more information on motivating employees, see Chapter 9.

"Some people think, 'Well, this is an easy business; I'll just hire someone and go play golf every day,'" says Paul Donovan, former vice president of marketing and sales with PWS, a distributor of laundry equipment. "It doesn't work that way."

The Down Payment

You may not need a lot of free time or experience to run a laundry, but you do need a pile of cash. Whether you buy an existing laundry business or build a new one, you can expect to pay between $50,000 and $1 million. A typical laundromat, if such a thing exists, would be a 2,000-square-foot, relatively modest store in a shopping center. For one of these, you are looking at paying between $200,000 and $500,000.

"It is a capital-intensive business," says Brian Wallace of the Coin Laundry Association. If you build a laundry, half the start-up costs are the price of equipment, he says, and half are remodeling the space and installing equipment. But take heart: Some laundry owners have received loans from banks. In addition, equipment manufacturers and distributors will finance the cost of equipment.

The Land of Lost Coins

You may hear customers complain that they put money into a machine and the machine didn't work. Naturally, you want to keep your customers happy, so you need to refund their money as quickly as possible. One way to do this is to post your phone number in the store and have customers call if they lose money. Alternatively, you can have them drop notes in a box.

Brian De Coster, who owns four unattended laundromats in and around Iowa City, Iowa, has set up drop boxes in his stores along with a stack of tickets and instructions on what to do if a customer loses money. The tickets have two parts. On one part of the ticket, the customer writes his name and address and the amount of money he lost. This part of the ticket goes in the drop box. The other part, which reads, "Broken," gets placed on the offending machine.

How do you know customers are telling the truth? That's a risk you might want to take. The refund won't cost you much, and if the same customer asks for more than a few refunds, then you can be suspicious. De Coster says that he's usually able to verify when someone has lost money. For example, if a customer claims she lost $5 in the change machine, he knows she's telling the truth because he'll find a jammed fiver in the machine when he opens it up. He adds that he hasn't found that anyone has tried to take advantage. He says, "A lot of times I think people are just interested in getting the problem fixed."

The Daily Routine

So what's it really like to own a laundry business? Whether you do all the work yourself or hire an attendant or a janitor, there are tasks you will need to take care of on a daily basis. You will need to open and close your store promptly each day, clean it, collect money, and fill vending and change machines. You will also need to keep track of which machines are being used and how often.

Those laundry owners who have employees will have other duties, too. They'll be hiring and supervising those employees and overseeing additional services such as wash-and-fold. See Chapter 9 for information on providing extra services and overseeing employees.

The Hours You Keep

Laundries are generally open between 6 A.M. and 10 P.M. seven days per week. Because weekends are usually the busiest days for laundries, you should definitely keep your doors open on Saturdays and Sundays. In some instances, you may want to adopt alternate hours, especially if the market you serve or the location of your store lends itself to having open doors at other times of the day.

Smart Tip

Tip...

When cleaning your store, check the insides of the machines to make sure something left in a pocket didn't spill out and create a mess.

De Coster keeps his stores open 24 hours per day. Three of his four laundromats are in a college town, and students are notorious for keeping odd hours. "You've got the machines; you've already paid the money for the machines and the rent and everything else," he reasons. Because his laundry is unattended, he doesn't have to pay employees to stay up all night with his store.

O'Connell keeps most of his stores open 24 hours as well. "The biggest problem we had was turning customers away," he says. "Customers would come in late and employees would want to be leaving, so it was easier just to stay open."

Other laundry owners we interviewed base their hours on surrounding businesses. Dave and Kris Anderson, who own an unattended laundry in New Glarus, Wisconsin, keep their store open daily from 5:30 A.M. to 10:30 P.M. They chose those hours because they're the same hours the nearby gas station is open. "We feel it's working out perfectly," Dave says. "If we had kept it open later, we might have had more vandalism."

Yet other owners consider their employees' convenience. "We didn't want to be open late at night," says Collette Clarkson, whose laundry, The Last Load, is open from 6 A.M. to 10 P.M. "And it's tough to find people to work those hours."

Your first duty of the day is to open your store, and you must be on time because your customers may plan their days around getting their laundry done at certain times. You can avoid having to be at your store early in the morning and late at night by installing an automatic lock system on a timer. A typical system like this will cost you between $1,000 and $1,500.

Dave and Kris Anderson installed an automatic system in their store. "It opens itself and locks itself," Dave says. The lights are also on a timer. Since both Dave and Kris have other jobs, the system has been invaluable to them.

At night, of course, you must close down and lock up. If you want all the customers to be gone by 10 P.M., you should consider locking the door at 8:30 P.M., leaving enough time for the last loads of laundry to be finished. You can either let customers out yourself or install a lock system that allows them to leave but prevents others from coming inside.

Scrub-a-Dub-Dub

Why do people visit a laundromat? They want clean clothes. As obvious as this may be, the operative word here is clean. No one wants to fold clothes in a pile of dust and cigarette ashes or place clothes in a dryer coated with lipstick (it happens). "Just make your place look nice and bright and clean," advises Brian De Coster.

The first order of business for you or an employee you hire is to clean your store thoroughly, at least once a day. This will take about two to three hours. You or your employee will need to do the following:

- Mop the floors
- Wipe down the machines
- Clean the soap dispensers in your front-load washers
- Wash off the folding tables
- Clean the bathroom
- Empty the trash
- Wash the windows
- Clean the vending machines, change machines, and video game screens

Dollar Stretcher

You can buy a stainless steel cleaner from your distributor to wipe down those stainless steel machines, or you can use a simple solution of ammonia and water. Wash with some clean rags and wipe the machines down when you're done. If you want to polish them, just use baby oil.

The best time to clean is after customers have gone—that way you or your employees can clean more efficiently. You'll also avoid the risk of customers slipping on wet floors or tripping over cleaning equipment. If you have a large or busy store, however, you may find that it requires cleaning twice a day. You can wipe down the machines and folding tables easily while customers are in the store, but save the floor for after they've left or for a slow period of the day.

Collecting Coins

One chore you're not likely to delegate to an employee is collecting money from the machines. If you have a card system (see Chapter 7 for more on card systems), your job is much easier. All you'll have to do is empty the card machine of the bills, count them and deposit them in the bank.

But if you have a coin laundry, you'll need to empty each machine, preferably daily. You'll want to pull (take out the coins) from one type of machine at a time so you can determine how often your customers are using each type of machine. Put a bag in one of your laundry baskets and roll it from machine to machine, starting with the top-loaders. Count these coins and record how much money you made on this type of machine, then follow the same procedure with the front-loaders and the dryers.

Bright Idea

If you don't have a coin counter, but you want to know how much a bag of quarters is worth, weigh them. One pound of quarters equals approximately $20.

For recording purposes, you should use a chart similar to the "Equipment Use Chart" we've provided on page 18. Draw up a chart with seven rows, one for each day of the week, and columns for each type and size of equipment: top-loaders, front-loaders, dryers, and vending machines. Then record in your chart how much money you withdraw every day. We'll discuss what to do with the information later in this chapter.

You should refill the change machine in your store on a daily basis, too. When it's empty, your customers can't do their laundry, and they'll go elsewhere. If it's empty more than a few times, they may never return. No one wants to lug several loads of laundry to a laundromat, only to find they can't get change. De Coster says if his change machine runs out, "that's like shooting myself in the foot. I check the change machine at least once a day."

Safety Comes First

It's usually best to empty machines on a daily basis. You can do this once or twice a week instead, but you risk losing more money in case of theft or robbery. When you pull once a day, the most you'll lose is one day's take. When you pull coins (or bills in the case of card machines and change machines), there are a number of preventive measures you should take to ensure your safety:

- Never try to pull coins or bills when no one's in the store. You're handling lots of cash, and you don't want to leave yourself vulnerable.

- Try to vary the time that you collect money. If you pull coins the same time every day, someone could plan ahead and lie in wait to rob you.

- Don't use a bank bag to collect money from your store. A bank bag says to potential thieves, "I'm full of money; steal me." Put the money in a lunch cooler, briefcase or purse—anything that doesn't look conspicuous.

- Deposit the money in the bank as quickly as possible. While this should be common sense, it's worth mentioning. Once you've taken care to collect the money from your machines safely, you don't want to put yourself at additional risk of robbery by carrying it with you any longer than necessary.

Let Us Vend

The last bit of daily business in your store is restocking the vending machines. If you own your own soda and snack machines, you will need to make sure they're full every day. If you contract with a vending company, they'll worry about filling them.

The most important vending machine in your store will likely be the soap vending machine, and since these machines are relatively inexpensive and rarely break, you should buy your own. Make sure it is properly stocked every day. Many customers will bring their own soap, but those who don't will expect to find soap available.

Equipment Use Chart

Use this chart to record how much money you've collected from each type of machine in your store. This will help you to keep track of which machines are getting the most use so you can find the best equipment mix for your store.

For the week of: _____

	Top-loaders	20-pound front-loaders	35-pound front-loaders	50-pound front-loaders	Dryers	Soap vending machine
Sunday						
Monday						
Tuesday						
Wednesday						
Thursday						
Friday						
Saturday						

An empty soap machine is almost as bad as an empty change machine—it will cause you to lose business.

Keeping Track

When you have completed the daily in-store duties, you'll need to take care of some additional office work. Many laundry owners do this at home, though some may find it easier to work in a rented office or at the laundromat if they have space. Owners with other businesses, such as Brian De Coster with the Iowa City, Iowa, laundries and the equipment rental business, can take care of everything in one office.

Smart Tip

Tip...

You may find that the soap dispensers in your front-load washers are caking with soap scum that's nearly as hard as stone. The scum is from soda ash, used as filler in inexpensive detergents. Try using a brush with hard bristles to remove the deposits. If that doesn't work, you can purchase a commercial descaler.

At your office, you'll need to take care of your accounting (we'll cover this in detail in Chapter 11) and track equipment usage by customers in your store. It's important to record how often each type of machine is used so that you can determine if you've got the right mix of equipment. For example, if you find that your front-loaders are getting six turns per day (the number of times a machine is used each day) and your top-loaders only two, you may need to add front-loaders and remove some top-loaders. Your customers are likely waiting for the front-loaders and possibly going elsewhere, so you could be losing money.

It's probably easiest to track machine use weekly, using the record of money you collect on a daily basis. If you collect weekly, you can record the money you make each week. As you accumulate these records, you should convert them to monthly figures so that you can calculate your net income by subtracting your monthly expenses from your gross monthly income. As with any business, you need to keep close tabs on income and expenses. With a laundry, you need to keep track of how much money each machine takes in and what each machine costs you (more on this in Chapter 11). Over time, you will be able to determine what equipment mix is best for your customers and your bottom line.

Next up: In Chapter 3, we'll take you through the ins and outs of market research. We'll also discuss how to put together a mission statement for your business.

Locating
Your Market

One of the most important steps in start-
ing a successful business is to make sure you do a thorough job
of researching the market. Don't skimp when it comes to
researching the laundry industry. You'll be investing hundreds
of thousands of dollars in purchasing or starting a new laundromat, so you want to make sure it's a good investment. You

need to know who your customers are, where they are, and what kind of competition you will face. The answers to these questions will be important in framing your business's purpose or mission statement. In this chapter, we'll focus on how to research the market and choose a good location for your laundry business.

Location, Location, Location

We've all heard the mantra "location, location, location" when it comes to real estate. This mantra is vastly more important when you're purchasing a laundromat, or starting a new one, than when you're looking for a home. Don't let this mantra slip out of your mind for one second while you are researching locations. In fact, you should make sure to repeat it several times a day. A good location is extremely important for a laundry.

"If you have a good location and you run your laundry right, you cannot fail," says laundry consultant Lionel Bogut. "It's all about location."

Laundry users head to the most convenient laundry. Customers aren't going to drag 30 pounds of laundry an extra half mile because they like the channel your TV is set to. They're also not likely to drive 30 minutes out of their way because they like the look of your machines. After all, the product—clean clothes—is the same no matter where they take their filled hampers. The California Coin Laundry Association estimates that 80 percent of your customers will use your laundry because of its location. Simply put: You need to be where your customers are.

Who Goes There?

When you're considering purchasing a laundromat, or you're thinking of leasing a site and building a new one, the first thing to do is take a good look at the surrounding neighborhood. Your customers will be people who don't have washers and dryers in their homes. For the most part, this means apartment-dwellers. But it also means people who rent houses, and lower-income folks who can't afford machines. So your best bet is to buy or open a laundromat in a low- to middle-income area surrounded by apartment buildings. "Usually with a laundromat you want at least 40 percent in that area to be renters," says Paul Donovan, formerly of laundry equipment distributor PWS. "That's where you are going to make your money."

Some homeowners with washers and dryers in their homes will use your laundry on occasion for large items or take advantage of your wash-and-fold service. However, they won't do this frequently enough to justify placing a laundromat in a well-heeled neighborhood full of single-family houses.

Besides looking at areas full of renters, you'll want to purchase or develop a laundromat in an area that has many families with children. Not only are there more clothes to wash in larger families, but children tend to soil clothing more quickly (theirs as well as their parents'). Other regular laundromat customers include students and seniors, who tend to live in smaller quarters and often don't have laundry equipment in their homes.

Finally, look at how the neighborhood is changing. Are large, older homes being converted into apartments? That's a good sign. Or are developers kicking out the renters, razing the buildings and replacing them with luxury lofts? That's a bad sign.

Bright Idea

If you're thinking of opening or purchasing a laundry in an area that attracts tourists, remember that vacationers need clean clothes, too. An ideal location would be one that's accessible to both the year-round crowd and the tourists.

The Hard Facts

Once you've scouted out the neighborhood of your future laundromat, you'll need to go in search of some hard demographics. Your intuition may tell you the location is right, but when you're investing several hundred thousand dollars in one store, you'll want as much information as you can get. Demographics will give you the ages and income levels of the residents in the area, whether they rent or own property, how many children they have, and how the neighborhood is changing.

You can order census information from the government, from a demographic service, or from the Coin Laundry Association (see the Appendix for contact information). Laundry equipment distributors can also supply you with demographic information. Check out page 24 for a sample of the demographic information you might gather for a particular area.

Smart Tip

Tip...

You can get general demographics from the U.S. Census Bureau. Check out their web site at www.census.gov. Click on "State & County Quick Facts"; choose your state and then your county or city. You can get general information about income levels, population growth, and home ownership for your city or county.

So let's review: A "good" neighborhood for a laundry has lots of renters with large families living on lower incomes or lots of young, single people who rent. But also look at how the statistics for the neighborhood have changed over the years. If the number of renters has dropped and incomes are rising, that's likely to continue and may not bode well for your laundromat. However, if the opposite is true, you may be looking at a growing customer base.

As stated above, most customers are going to visit the laundromat that's most convenient to them. If you're thinking of an urban location where customers are going to carry their laundry to your store, you can expect them to walk

MapFacts Demographic Summary: 2004
5341 N LINCOLN AVE: CHICAGO,IL 60625
0.5 Mi Ring (Site located at 41.9788, 87.6926)

Scan/US, Inc.
06/14/2005

Legend
- ☐ Site Ringareas (MG04)
- ■ '03 Census Places 10K-<50K
- Places < 10K
- Places 10K - 49.9K
- Places 50K - 499.9K
- Places 500K+

0   0.5   1   1.5   2
⊿N Scale: 1" = 1.61 miles

Population	**16,554**		**Households**	**6,073**	
In Group Quarters	306	1.8%	Average Household Size	2.7	
			Family Households	**3,968**	65.3%
Race: White	10,011	60.5%	Average Family Size	3.3	
Black	511	3.1%	**Non-Family Households**	**2,105**	34.7%
American Indian	43	0.3%	Average Non-Fam HH Size	1.5	
Asian/Pacific Islander	3,655	22.1%			
Other Race	2,335	14.1%	**Households by Income**		
Hispanic Origin	4,023	24.3%	$0 - $24,999	1,595	26.3%
			$25,000 - $49,999	1,915	31.5%
Sex: Male	8,094	48.9%	$50,000 - $74,999	1,219	20.1%
Female	8,460	51.1%	$75,000 - $99,999	662	10.9%
			$100,000 - $149,999	474	7.8%
Age: < 5 Years	1,158	7.0%	$150,000 +	209	3.4%
5 - 9 Years	1,005	6.1%			
10 - 14 Years	1,001	6.0%	**Average HH Income**	**$54,916**	
15 - 19 Years	955	5.8%	**Median HH Income**	**$43,888**	
20 - 24 Years	1,013	17.0%	**Per Capita Income**	**$20,295**	
25 - 34 Years	2,820	16.3%			
35 - 44 Years	2,695	13.4%	**Vehicles Available**	**6,930**	
45 - 54 Years	2,216	9.6%	Average Vehicles/HH	1.1	
55 - 64 Years	1,585	6.2%			
65 - 74 Years	1,030	4.1%	**Total Housing Units**	**6,312**	
75 - 84 Years	677	2.4%	Owner Occupied	2,240	35.5%
85+ Years	401		Renter Occupied	3,833	60.7%
Median Age	**36.3**		Vacant	239	3.8%

www.scanus.com   Source: 2004 Scan/US Estimates   06/14/2005

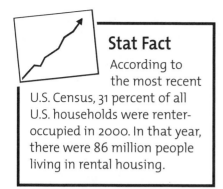

Stat Fact

According to the most recent U.S. Census, 31 percent of all U.S. households were renter-occupied in 2000. In that year, there were 86 million people living in rental housing.

no more than half a mile. So if you're looking at an urban location, get demographic information within a half mile of the location you're considering.

In a suburban location—usually in a strip mall with parking—you can expect customers to drive no more than five miles to your store. A rural location, however, will draw customers from as far as ten miles away. So if you will locate your laundry in either a suburban or rural locale, you should look at the demographics within five or ten miles of the site.

If you are considering purchasing or opening a laundry in an area that is growing, visit the city, township or county the site is located in and ask for the General Plan. The plan will show what areas are slated for businesses, what areas are designated for low- to middle-income apartments, and what areas will be developed as single-family houses. You'll want to be sure your laundry is in an area that will fit with the kinds of people who use laundromats—primarily low- to middle-income apartment-dwellers.

The Competition

Laundromats aren't like antique stores or boutique shops, which offer distinctive, specialty items. You may find these specialty stores in fairly close proximity to each other because shoppers like to browse several stores during one shopping trip. Laundromats, on the other hand, are like grocery stores. They're usually spaced apart every so many miles, since customers pretty much get the same results from each store.

Generally, you don't want to build a new laundromat near other laundromats. You also don't want to buy a laundromat that has too many competitors close by. If you do, the competition will be too intense, and you may end up dropping your prices so low that you won't be able to get out of the red. As we mentioned in Chapter 1, the laundry business is a mature industry. Unless your region of the country is growing, it's likely there are already enough laundries in the neighborhood you're considering.

However, don't be discouraged. If it seems like the laundry market is saturated in the area you're considering, be sure to take a good look at the competition. If the stores are run down or located in high-crime areas, many customers may be eager to visit a clean, new store—one with properly working equipment, a functioning change machine, and amenities like computer terminals and free coffee. Also consider how many customers are using the store: If there's always a wait for machines or the store is packed just before closing, there may be plenty of business to go around.

Finally, if you're offering services that differ from what other stores have to offer, such as wash-and-fold or dry cleaning, you may have a leg up on the competition. Tom

▲

Leavitt, owner of Darcies Laundry in the Seattle area, opened all three of his laundries in locations that were near other laundromats. But the existing laundries were older and smaller, while his offered enough machines to ensure customers wouldn't have to wait. "In all of our locations, the competition that was there has closed," Leavitt says.

When you're choosing a location for your laundromat, consider nearby businesses. Busy people (and that's just about all of us) like to do their errands all at once. Having a drug store, a sandwich shop, a dry cleaner, and a supermarket near your location lets customers do everything in one fell swoop. They can pick up a sandwich for lunch and eat it while they do their laundry, as well as leave their dry cleaning with you, refill a prescription, and do the food shopping for the week—all without having to move the car.

Make sure the businesses surrounding your store are thriving and well kept. A shopping mall that's on the decline won't attract the traffic you need. And being near a string of run-down stores will make your laundromat look run down as well. You should also steer clear of businesses that attract rowdy customers, such as bars or video arcades. Your customers may be scared away, and you'll likely have more of a problem with vandalism.

> **Tip...**
>
> **Smart Tip**
>
> If your lease includes periodic rent increases, calculate what the rent will be for the last month you're there. Then do your best to project what your income will be at that time. Make sure you can still afford the rent at the end of the lease.

What's In a Name?

Traditionally, laundromats have been called just that— "Laundromat." Some are "Coin-Op Laundry," "Wash & Dry," or, in some Spanish-speaking areas, "Lavandería." While you want to make sure the name you give your laundry reflects the fact that it's a laundry, there's no reason you can't give your business more individuality.

Tom Leavitt named his Seattle-area laundry chain "Darcies Laundry" after a friend. He and his partner didn't want to call their store simply "Laundromat" or "Wash and Dry" and have customers say, "I'm going to go to that laundry that's across the street from the grocery store on the corner of 44th." They chose to spell the name with "ie" rather than "y" so they could incorporate their daisy logo—as the dot over the letter "i."

Collette Clarkson named her Evans, Colorado, laundry "The Last Load" to lend a touch of humor to the business. She says, "We thought it was funny, like, 'Whew, that's the last load.'"

Hidden Rivals

Keep in mind that some apartment buildings, especially larger complexes, have their own laundry facilities. If they are in good condition and offer enough machines, the residents will do their laundry there.

If you think some of the apartment complexes near your potential site might already have washers and dryers, call them and find out. Larger apartment buildings (the ones most likely to have laundry facilities) usually have a rental office with a number listed in the phone book. When you call, don't forget to find out how many machines they have available for their renters. If they have just one or two washers, many of the residents will end up using a laundromat rather than wait for a machine to become available.

When there aren't enough machines, says Donovan, the residents aren't going to want to go down to the facility and wait for several other renters to do their laundry first. "At a laundromat, they can do all their wash at once," he says. "They feel more comfortable going to a place, getting five washers going, and getting all the wash done for the week."

Other Pieces of the Puzzle

Even if the demographics you have gathered seem favorable, and you've decided you can live with the competition, you may find yourself back at the drawing board if your location doesn't meet other important criteria. Other pieces of the puzzle, like zoning requirements and lease agreements, have to fall into place for a location to be promising.

Zoned Out

The first step to take when you find a location you like is to check with the local municipality to ensure that it's zoned for a laundromat. If it's not, you're back to the drawing board—unless you can persuade the local authority to change the zoning. If you have found an existing laundry that you want to buy, the previous owner should have checked this out already.

Beware!
If the site of your laundry-to-be is in a strip mall, you can expect to pay a share of the expenses for maintaining the common area. These can include fees for snow removal, landscaping, management, and taxes. Ask about these if you don't see them in the lease.

In addition to zoning requirements, you need to find out what fees you will have to pay for sewer connection (to hook up washers to sewer lines) and sewer and wastewater fees. As we'll discuss further in Chapter 5, sewer connection fees can be prohibitively expensive; however, they can also be applied sporadically, says Brian Wallace, president and CEO of the Coin Laundry Association. "On one side of the street there may be no impact fees, and down the block a little ways, there may be fees of several thousand dollars per washer," Wallace says. The only way to know what your fees will be like is to check with the local water district.

You'll also have to think about how difficult it will be to turn your leased space into a laundry, if it's not already one. You will need to make sure you have at least a two-inch connection for water and gas. You'll also need to check that the water service is metered. Making these upgrades can be expensive. Check with your distributor and your contractor (see Chapter 6 for more on experts) about the work that will need to be done to your site before it's ready to be a laundry. Your contractor will know what's needed to remodel the space and how much it will cost; your distributor will know what connections or utility requirements you will need for the equipment you plan to buy.

Lease, Lease, Lease

So you've determined that the location is good; the zoning allows a laundry at the site; the connection fees are low; and there's adequate water, gas and electricity at this site. You can stop saying, "location, location, location." Now you must start saying, "lease, lease, lease."

The importance of a good lease is second only to location. Rent will be one of your biggest expenses, so make sure the rent is something you can afford. Also remember that a laundry is not a consulting business, which can move offices frequently with little expense as long as the consultant has a cellular phone. As stated previously, the success of a laundry is almost completely dependent on location. So if your landlord kicks you out of the building, all you have left is used equipment. And that's usually not worth more than a few thousand dollars.

"You can't pick up and move a coin laundry," emphasizes Wallace. "Leases are very important. When the lease is over, you're out of business." So you'll need to negotiate a long lease—at least 10 years, 15 or 20 years if you can get it. If you're buying a laundromat, make sure that the lease is transferable and that you have at least 10 years left on it. It's likely the landlord will raise the rent as time goes by, often according to inflation, so you can expect to pay more over the course of 20 years. That's OK as long as the increases are reasonable. You just want to make sure you won't be kicked out.

When you are drawing up the lease agreement, make sure you can have vending machines, food sales, or any other special services you plan to offer. Some leases may forbid ancillary income. Be especially careful about clauses that terminate the lease under special situations. These include fires or floods, or a life interest (this means that if the building owner dies, the lease is over).

Because the lease is so important to a laundromat, you should seek help from a real estate attorney when negotiating it. Certainly have an attorney review the lease before you sign it!

Park it Here

If you are looking at locations in a densely populated urban area where people will be walking from their homes to the laundromat, you don't have to worry about parking. You can skip this section. However, if you're considering a suburban or rural location, you must pay close attention. It is vitally important for your store to have adequate parking. We are back to that convenience thing—if it's not easy to park the car, customers are not going to use your laundry.

Many suburban laundry owners find themselves operating a store in a strip mall. A large part of the reason is that strip malls have plenty of parking. But don't just look at the parking lot in the middle of the weekday and figure there's plenty of room. Drive into the parking lot during the laundry rush hours—evenings and weekends—and see how easily you can find a parking space. If you have to wait 15 minutes before you can pull your car into a spot, you can bet your customers will drive off to another laundry long before 15 minutes are up.

Also think about how accessible a potential site is from the road. If your future customers have to make a left turn into heavy traffic without a protected signal, they may drive on. And if they have to risk their lives to pull out of the parking lot, they'll try another store next time.

> **Tip...**
>
> **Smart Tip**
>
> Sign research has shown that certain colors are easier to read at a distance. Here are the top five color combinations:
>
> 1. Black letters on yellow background
> 2. Black letters on white background
> 3. Yellow letters on black background
> 4. White letters on blue background
> 5. Yellow letters on blue background

See and Be Seen

While you need to make sure your customers can drive or easily walk to your laundromat, you must also be sure that passersby can see it. A spot in an alley with good parking might work for a hairdresser who gets most of her business through referrals, but it won't work for laundry owners.

Most customers find laundromats because they see them on the street. They find them when they're walking to the grocery store or driving to work, and they decide to give them a try. While word-of-mouth and advertising will also help to draw in customers, visibility is probably your best advertisement. Make sure the site you're investigating can be seen easily from the road. Drive or walk by it from different directions and at different times of the day and note whether it stands out.

If your potential site is in a suburban or rural area, you'll likely do better if the site is on a busy street rather than a quiet, out-of-the-way road. In urban areas, where there is plenty of foot traffic, you'll want to think more about a central location that will draw residents from the immediate vicinity. A corner spot is often helpful because people can see your store from more than one street.

Check with the municipality where you will open your laundry to find out about signage regulations. Cities and counties have different rules about how big signs can be and whether lighting is allowed. Also check with your landlord: Strip malls and business complexes may have rules regarding signs, too.

In general, the larger and brighter your sign is, the better. You should try not to clutter signs with too many words or phrases. And make sure the words "laundry," "laundromat," or "wash" are included in your sign so there's no danger of customers mistaking your store for another type of business.

On a Mission

Once you've decided to pursue the laundry business and have found a suitable location, be sure to write a mission statement to help guide you in designing and developing your store. A mission statement is a brief description of your business's purpose. It should include what region your business serves, who your customers are and what services you will offer.

For example, one mission statement might be, "Our mission is to provide a fun, safe and clean location for Tallahassee residents to wash their clothes." Or: "Our mission is to offer a store with enough quality laundry equipment for southwest Portland residents to be able to do their laundry quickly and at a fair price."

An accurate mission statement helps you focus as you grow your business, and it helps your employees understand their work goals. Print the statement in large type on a poster and display it in a place where you and your attendants will see it every day. Take a look at the worksheet we've provided on page 31 for developing an effective mission statement.

In addition to finding your customers and a good location, you have yet another major decision to make—will you buy an existing laundromat or build a new one in a leased space? In Chapter 4, we will show you how to approach this question and make the best choice for your new business.

Developing Your Mission Statement

Use this worksheet to start developing your mission statement. Your statement should clearly define the following:

○ *Your geographic area.* From what area do you expect to draw customers?

○ *Your customers.* What types of customers will use your laundromat—students, seniors, vacationers, families?

○ *The services you will offer.* Will you provide wash-and-fold, alterations, manicures, or any other services?

○ *The image you want to project.* What kind of atmosphere will you provide for your customers? Will you have a theme, such as "The Old West" or "Outer Space," for your laundry? Do you want to be known as the largest laundry in town, the laundry with friendly attendants, or the laundry that's fun to visit?

Mission Statement for

_____

(your business name)

_____

_____

_____

_____

_____

_____

_____

_____

_____

_____

_____

_____

_____

To Buy or Build?

One of the first decisions you'll have to make after you've decided to join the laundry owners' club is whether you want to buy an existing laundry business or build a new one in a leased storefront. Your decision will be based partly on personal preference. Do you want to take a risk on a new, untried store? Or do you want to take over one with a proven track record? It's very likely that market conditions will determine which route you end up choosing. In this chapter, we'll help you decide when it's right to build a laundromat and when it makes more sense to buy an existing business. We'll also steer you through the buying process.

When to Build

When is building a new laundromat the best choice? As we've mentioned, most areas of the country have all the laundromats they need. However, there are cities and counties that are growing rapidly and potentially need new laundromats. If the population growth in an area includes an increase in the customer base that most often uses laundries (low- to middle-income renters), building a new laundromat might make more sense than buying one.

Areas experiencing a population boom aren't the only places in need of a laundromat, though. There are also a few neighborhoods that just don't have one. Either a laundromat business never made it there or a laundry closed. Dave and Kris Anderson, who own Alpine Laundry in New Glarus, Wisconsin, opened their business several years after the laundromat in their town shut down. Everyone knew the town needed a new laundry. "It became kind of a hot topic around here," Dave says. "Two other people were thinking about doing it. It was a race to see who bought the land and was first." Whatever the situation in your town, just make sure there are enough customers to support your business.

Another reason you might take a chance on building a new laundromat is if you think your business can draw customers from existing laundromats. Maybe you have a new gimmick you want to promote, such as a combination nightclub/laundry; perhaps you will offer a variety of services, such as wash-and-fold, dry cleaning, or clothing repair. Or you may plan to build a large laundry with plenty of machines, a children's play area, televisions and a snack bar. If the laundries in your neighborhood are small and offer no amenities, customers may choose your business over the competition because their stay will be more pleasant and they won't have to wait for machines.

If you decide to go this route, your decision should be based on solid market research and not just a hunch. Find out if there is a sufficient customer base to draw business from and whether they want the atmosphere or amenities that you will offer.

Your decision to build rather than buy may depend on what's for sale. If the laundries for

> **Tip...**
>
> ## Smart Tip
> Ask to see the general plan for your city or county. This will have information on how much the area is expected to grow, where it will grow, and what type of housing will be built.

sale in your area have too many problems, or if none are for sale, building may be your only option—provided that your area can support a new laundry.

Finally, you may want to build if you feel uncomfortable taking over a business. Buying an existing laundry is a little like buying a used car—you're never really sure why the owner is selling. In addition, you don't know what kinds of problems you may inherit if you take over somebody's lease.

Beware!

If you're building a laundry, be aware that regular insurance covering property and casualty will not cover you during the construction phase. To cover yourself in case of fire, theft, or other damage while you're building your store, purchase builders' risk insurance.

Building 101

Most laundry owners who build a laundromat do so by leasing a storefront, remodeling the space, and installing equipment—rather than constructing a store from the ground up. If you decide to go this route, you'll need to negotiate a lease,

How Big Can You Go?

You may be motivated to build a huge store to make a bigger profit or to draw in customers who don't want to wait for machines at smaller stores. Just remember that a big store is going to cost you—not only in construction costs and the price of equipment, but also in the rent you will have to pay to keep the machines waiting around to be used.

If you're in a large metropolitan area with good access to low- and middle-income rental housing, you can probably get away with a large store. Customers will skip other laundries to visit yours if it's large and has a pleasant atmosphere. But if the customer base you expect to draw from is small, don't build any larger than necessary.

Cindy Patel opened a 6,000-square-foot laundry in Shelby, North Carolina, a small town that already had a number of laundries. A year after opening, she's still struggling to break even, partly because her loans were so large.

Before you buy or build a laundry, determine how much laundry you can expect your customers to bring in and size your store accordingly. Start by reviewing a demographics report for your area. Then talk to your distributor or consultant about what an appropriate size might be for your store.

hire a contractor, choose a distributor, and promote the store. Your distributor should be able to tell you if you've found a good location for your laundry. We'll cover the basics of choosing contractors and distributors in Chapter 6.

Keep in mind that if you decide to build a laundromat, you will have an advantage over your competitors if you build a much larger store. Although your competition can often add amenities, such as wash-and-fold service or televisions, they can't add to the size of their stores. This means they can't compete with the number of machines you'll have, and they likely can't add a snack bar or offer services that take up space, such as dry-cleaning drop-off and pickup. "It makes sense to build if you put in a nice big new laundry," says laundry consultant Lionel Bogut. "People know they can always come to your store and find a washer."

Tom Leavitt, who opened laundries in three cities in the Seattle area, found that his chain has done very well by drawing customers looking for nicer equipment and more amenities. The chain offers a kids' play area, many televisions, full-time attendants and a card system. He says, "Our stores are very convenient, they're big, there are a lot of machines, they're clean, it's a friendly environment, and you can get in and out of there as fast as possible."

When to Buy

There are several good reasons to consider buying an existing laundry business rather than building a new one. If there isn't the customer base for another laundry in your town or your water district imposes such high sewer connection fees that it's not practical to build, buying an existing laundry may be your only option.

In some areas of the country, sewer connection fees are as high as $8,000 per washer. That means if you build a 40-washer laundromat, you'll have to pay more than $300,000 just for the installation of your washers. These fees can double the price of building a new laundromat, making it far more attractive to buy an existing one instead.

Finally, you might choose to buy a laundromat if you don't want the hassle of starting a business from scratch and worrying about whether it will take off. An existing store is already up and running, and it has a proven track record.

If You Buy

Possibly the most important factor you'll need to consider when buying a laundry business is where it's located. As we discussed in Chapter 3, there are many factors that will go into finding just the right location. Your laundry must be close to the homes of its likely customers—low- to middle-income renters—and you must be able to negotiate a long lease at a good price. It should be far enough removed from the competition, unless your business will have an edge on the competition. You should also consider a site that is visible to potential customers, easy to renovate (if that's your plan), and in a place where you can provide good parking.

You can find laundries for sale in the newspaper. Many distributors (the people who sell you equipment) also act as brokers. They'll sell a laundry to you on behalf of the owner.

Smart Tip

To keep customers from sitting on machines and folding tables, you should provide chairs where they can sit and wait for their laundry to finish.

Distributors will also build new laundries themselves and sell them to new owners. They'll develop a property, install the equipment and add all the extras, such as seats and laundry carts. Then they'll work out the expenses and expected income for the store and give that to you in a sheet called a pro forma (to see an example, turn to page 38). If you decide to buy a new laundromat from a distributor, you still need to research the location carefully yourself. Remember, it's in the best interest of the distributor to sell you the store.

Kicking the Tires

Once you have found a laundromat you're interested in buying, you'll need to investigate it as if you were buying a used car: look under the hood, check the mileage and research the model. Find out why the owner wants to sell; if there's a good reason, you

---

All Yours

You won't have to worry about a lease that will expire, a landlord who's particular about changes, or any common-area expenses when you own the property your laundry is on. While it's not a requirement, there are advantages to this strategy if you can swing it.

Dave Anderson, who owns a laundromat in New Glarus, Wisconsin, with his wife, Kris, bought a piece of land in town and built a laundry on the property. Cindy Patel in Shelby, North Carolina, also purchased her building. While both entrepreneurs say they're struggling to pay off loans, neither has to worry about getting kicked out or facing rent hikes.

Unfortunately, this tactic won't work for every laundry owner. Some of the best places to locate a laundry—such as strip malls—aren't for sale or are prohibitively expensive.

Sample Pro Forma

PWS, Inc. makes a good faith effort to project income and expenses, but does not guarantee this projection and is not responsible for its accuracy. This is one of multiple sets of assumptions used for the purpose of CREDIT ANALYSIS ONLY. This analysis is for INTERNAL USE ONLY and is not a representation of expected cash flows. This analysis is NOT to be relied on for investment purposes.

Date Prepared: June 20, 2005
Laundry - Sample Laundry
Address - 1234 Main St.
City - Anytown, CA

INCOME AND EXPENSE STATEMENT

Income	Daily	Monthly
Washer-Dryer Income	$1,227.72	$37,445.31
Vending-Soap&Drinks	$100.00	$3,050.00
Wash, Dry, Fold	$28.00	$854.00
Other	$0.00	$0.00

DEBT SERVICE ANALYSIS

Sales Price:	$1,000,000	Term:	84
Down Payment:	$400,000	Interest Rate:	7.50%
Amount to be Financed:	$600,000	Mo. Payment:	$9,203
Finance % of Investment	40.00%		

Equipment

Equipment	Quantity	Vend Price	Turns per Day	Income
WASHERS				
Top Load	17	$1.30	4.5	$99.45
Horizon	0	$0.00	0.0	$0.00
20 lb	10	$2.00	4.5	$90.00
30 lb	20	$3.00	5.0	$300.00
40 lb	0	$0.00	0.0	$0.00
60 lb	8	$5.95	5.0	$238.00
80 lb	3	$7.95	5.0	$119.25
TUMBLERS				Total Wash Income $846.70
Stacks	25			
30 lb				
50 lb	8			Total Dry as a % of Wash $381.02
				Total Wash & Dry Income $1,227.72

10-Year Projection

Expenses	Price / Foot	Monthly	Year 1	Year 2	Year 3	Year 4	Year 5	Year 6	Year 7	Year 8	Year 9	Year 10
Total Income		$41,349	$496,192	$511,077	$526,410	$542,202	$558,468	$575,222	$592,479	$610,253	$628,561	$647,418
Base Rent	$1.56	6,000	72,005	72,005	72,005	72,005	82,805	82,805	82,805	82,805	82,805	95,226
R.E. Taxes	$0.10	384	4,608	4,746	4,889	5,035	5,186	5,342	5,502	5,667	5,667	5,667
R.E. Insurance	$0.05	192	2,304	2,373	2,444	2,518	2,593	2,671	2,751	2,834	2,834	2,834
R.E CAM	$0.01	38	461	475	489	504	519	534	550	567	584	601
Gas	11.00%	4,119	49,428	50,911	52,438	53,749	55,093	56,194	57,318	58,465	59,634	60,827
Water	9.00%	3,370	40,441	41,654	42,904	43,976	45,076	45,977	46,897	47,835	48,791	49,767
Electric	6.00%	2,247	26,961	27,769	28,603	29,318	30,051	30,652	31,265	31,890	32,528	33,178
Insurance		625	7,500	7,725	7,957	8,195	8,441	8,695	8,955	9,224	9,501	9,786
Personal Prop. Tax		0	0	1	1	1	1	1	1	1	1	1
Trash Collection		125	1,500	1,545	1,591	1,639	1,688	1,739	1,791	1,845	1,900	1,957
Vending costs		1,525	18,300	18,849	19,414	19,997	20,597	21,215	21,851	22,507	23,182	23,877
Parts and Repair		100	1,200	1,236	1,273	1,311	1,350	1,391	1,432	1,475	1,519	1,565
Fluff & Fold		128	1,537	1,583	1,631	1,672	1,713	1,748	1,818	1,855	1,892	1,892
Labor		3,931	47,174	48,590	50,047	51,299	52,581	53,633	54,705	55,799	56,915	58,054
Miscellaneous		413	4,962	5,111	5,264	5,422	5,585	5,752	5,925	6,103	6,286	6,474
Cards		500	6,000	6,180	6,365	6,525	6,688	6,821	6,958	7,097	7,239	7,384
Total Expenses		23,698	278,381	284,572	290,949	304,315	321,185	326,491	331,920	337,473	342,900	360,872
Cash Flow from Operations		17,651	217,811	226,505	235,461	237,887	237,283	248,731	260,559	272,780	285,660	286,546

Square Feet 3,840

CASH FLOW

	Year 1	Year 2	Year 3	Year 4	Year 5	Year 6	Year 7	Year 8	Year 9	Year 10
Cash flow from Operations *	217,811	226,505	235,461	237,887	237,283	248,731	260,559	272,780	285,660	286,546
Less Debt Service *	110,436	110,436	110,436	110,436	110,436	110,436	110,436	-	-	-
Less Secondary Debt Service	-	-	-	-	-	-	-	-	-	-
Net Cash flow after Debt Service	107,375	116,070	125,025	127,451	126,848	138,295	150,124	272,780	285,660	286,546

TAXABLE INCOME / LOSS

	Year 1	Year 2	Year 3	Year 4	Year 5	Year 6	Year 7	Year 8	Year 9	Year 10
Cash Flow Before Debt Service	217,811	226,505	235,461	237,887	237,283	248,731	260,559	272,780	285,660	286,546
Less Depreciation	116,152	178,552	111,992	72,056	72,056	41,792	12,152	12,152	12,152	12,152
Less Interest	42,703	37,445	31,778	25,672	19,092	12,000	$0	$0	$0	$0
Taxable Income/Loss	58,956	10,509	91,690	140,159	146,136	194,939	248,407	260,628	273,508	274,394

RETURN ON INVESTMENT

	Year 1	Year 2	Year 3	Year 4	Year 5	Year 6	Year 7	Year 8	Year 9	Year 10
Cash on Cash R.O.I.	27%	29%	31%	32%	32%	35%	38%	68%	71%	72%
Equity Build-up R.O.I.	17%	18%	20%	21%	23%	25%	28%	28%	28%	28%
Total R.O.I.	44%	47%	51%	53%	55%	59%	65%	96%	99%	99%

Note: The R.O.I. Analysis does not consider the tax consequence when the business is sold.

Annual Increases

	Year 2	Year 3	Year 4	Year 5	Year 6	Year 7	Year 8	Year 9	Year 10
Income	3.00%	3.00%	3.00%	3.00%	3.00%	3.00%	3.00%	3.00%	3.00%
Rent	0.00%	0.00%	0.00%	15.00%	0.00%	0.00%	0.00%	0.00%	15.00%
General Expenses	3.00%	3.00%	3.00%	3.00%	3.00%	3.00%	3.00%	3.00%	3.00%
Labor	3.00%	3.00%	2.50%	2.50%	2.00%	2.00%	2.00%	2.00%	2.00%

Other Income

Other Income	Daily
Vending (Soaps, Snacks, Drinks)	$100.00
Wash, Dry and Fold	$28.00
Miscellaneous Income - Net (Video Games etc)	$0.00
Total	$128.00

need to know what it is upfront. But beware that the owner may not tell you the real reasons for selling.

If you're buying from a distributor, remember that he or she is trying to make a sale, not give you a great business opportunity. The most important step is to make sure there is a customer base to support the laundry. The second thing is to determine the length of the lease on the laundry. If the owner has two years left on the lease, you know why he or she is selling—the business will be closed in two years. You'll want at least ten years on the lease. Ask to see a copy of the lease agreement.

Next, check with your city or county government about any construction slated for the neighborhood. Make sure there aren't any upcoming changes that would make the owner want to sell. A large new laundry chain next door could kill your business. So could a plan to raze the apartment complexes across the street and build high-end condominiums. You should also obtain current demographic information. Is the number of renters in the area stagnant or decreasing? Maybe that's why the owner is selling.

Take a tour of the store you are considering buying so you can see firsthand what sort of shape it's in. Call the owner of the store to arrange a time. Take a careful look at the "Pre-Purchase Laundry Evaluation" worksheet we've provided on page 40 to see what you'll need to inspect to cover all your bases.

When visiting the store, first look at the parking situation to see if customers have enough places to park. Then look in the customer area to get an overall impression of the store. Check whether any major repairs are needed for damaged floors, walls or ceilings. Think about the layout of the store: Is there enough room for customers to move laundry carts around? Is it open and visible from the street so vandals or thieves can't hide? Would it be possible to do some inexpensive renovating to improve the store?

Look in the back rooms where the water heaters and storage areas are. Go behind the dryers; check out the restroom. You'll want to make sure the store is well kept, even in the areas customers never see. These areas should be neat and free of lint buildup and water stains. If the owner can't keep the back areas in good condition, he or she may not be keeping the machines in good working order either.

This brings us to an important part of the inspection: Check the machines carefully to see that they're in good condition. If more than a few are broken, this shows that the owner is not keeping up with repairs—or that the machines are of poor quality. Ask the owner for documents stating the age of the equipment; don't just take his or her word for it. We've provided a list of "Warning Signs" on page 41 that you should look out for when you tour a prospective laundry business.

If you're new to the laundry business, it's a good idea to bring along someone experienced to evaluate the condition of the store. You can hire a consultant to give you an honest evaluation (see Chapter 6 for more on consultants and other experts). You can also ask another laundry owner to accompany you, or you can approach your regional laundry association for assistance.

Pre-Purchase Laundry Evaluation

When you take a tour of a laundromat for sale, take this worksheet and write down your impressions. These notes, along with the length of the lease, age of the equipment, and demographics, will help you determine what the laundromat is worth.

1. Parking: _____

_____

2. Visibility from street: _____

_____

3. Condition of floor: _____

_____

4. Condition of ceiling: _____

_____

5. Appearance of washers: _____

_____

6. Appearance of dryers: _____

_____

7. Washer-dryer ratio: _____

_____

8. Condition of vending machines: _____

_____

9. Condition of change machines: _____

_____

10. Layout of equipment: _____

_____

11. Condition of back rooms: _____

_____

12. Amenities: _____

_____

13. Temperature inside store: _____

_____

14. Overall atmosphere: _____

_____

15. Number of customers: _____

_____

Warning Signs Checklist

If you're considering buying a laundromat, the current owner is likely to paint a rosy picture of the store's condition. So you should inspect the store yourself and take note of any of the following warning signs:

- ❏ Cracked floor tiles or other damage to the floor
- ❏ Signs of vandalism to coin boxes or change machines
- ❏ More than a few machines out of order
- ❏ Water stains around washers
- ❏ Give in the drums of dryers and front-loaders
- ❏ Black dryer drums (indicating the coating has worn off)
- ❏ Burn or smoke marks in access doors of dryers
- ❏ Discoloration or burn marks on water heater
- ❏ Rust or discoloration of water heater exhaust ducts
- ❏ Water marks or water on the floor near the water heater
- ❏ Malfunctioning bill changer
- ❏ Vandalism in restroom

Crunching the Numbers

Once you've evaluated the condition of the store, you must find out how much the store is making. Again, don't take the owner's word for it. Ask for the following documents so you can evaluate the expenses involved in running the store:

- The lease agreement (to see the amount of rent and scheduled increases)
- Water bills
- Gas bills
- Electric bills
- Sewer bills
- Repair bills
- Employee payroll
- Insurance agreement
- Annual taxes
- Invoices for supplies

Don't forget the myriad other expenses you incur while running a business, such as trash

 Beware!

Laundry income peaks at certain times of the year. The first warm weather in the spring and the first cold weather in the fall result in an increase in business by as much as 20 percent. Be sure you adjust for this if you're evaluating a laundry during those times of the year.

removal, office supplies, advertising, telephone charges, cleaning supplies, association fees, and accounting.

Once you have a handle on expenses, you'll want to evaluate how much income the store generates. You know how much each customer pays to use a machine, so all you need to find out is how often each is used. The owner will tell you how many turns per day the machines get (the number of times each machine is used daily), but try to verify this figure by getting a few outside opinions. An experienced laundry owner, distributor, or consultant—someone who doesn't have a stake in selling you the store—may be able to tell you how many turns per day you can expect.

Another option is to visit the store yourself to research usage. Park yourself in the store for a full day and count the number of times each machine is used. Consider whether it's a slow day (midweek) or a busy one (weekend) and factor that into your estimate. This count will give you a general idea of what kind of income to expect. See the income and expense analyses in Chapter 11 for more on figuring out a store's net income.

> **Bright Idea**
> One way to determine how much money a laundry is taking in is to calculate the number of turns per day (the number of times a machine is used daily) based on water usage. Top-loaders and front-loaders of various sizes use a predictable amount of water. Check the California Coin Laundry Association web site to learn how to make this calculation (see the Appendix for contact information).

What's it Worth to You?

Once you have crunched the numbers and decided that the laundromat is making a heady enough profit, you'll need to determine whether the asking price is fair. This can be difficult because the value of a laundromat is subjective. A laundry may be worth more to you than to someone else because you own the sandwich shop next door and would like to merge them. On the other hand, you may be looking at several stores and have only so much money to spend, so you might be willing to pay less than other buyers.

Whatever your situation, you don't want to overpay. There's no need to shell out $300,000 when a laundry is worth only $200,000. So how do you determine a fair value for a laundromat? Some laundry owners figure that the value of a laundry is roughly equal to 50 times its monthly net income. So if a laundry is taking in $1,000 per month after expenses, it's worth $50,000. This amount assumes that the lease has 15 years left, the equipment is three years old, the neighborhood is stable, and the pricing and amenities are average. For more favorable conditions—a longer lease, a growing population of renters, new equipment—you should assume that the laundry is worth more than that. Likewise, for unfavorable conditions, such as machines in need of repair, lower income being generated and fewer amenities, you should assume that the store is worth less than this formula.

The Fixer-Upper

You may be able to find a good deal on a laundromat that has fallen into disrepair. If the owner hasn't kept the store neat and the machines in good condition, it's likely that customers have started to drift elsewhere. This reduces profits and in turn lowers the laundromat's value. With a little tender, loving care, you may be able to attract customers back to the store and turn the business around.

Your best deal is a laundry that needs a little spiffing up—new paint, new floors, a few new machines—but not major repairs. You'd be surprised how much more inviting the laundry can look with a few cosmetic treatments.

Tim O'Connell, who owns 24 laundries in the Syracuse, New York, area, says that while he usually builds a new laundry, he's purchased a few that were in good locations but hadn't been taken care of. "A lot of times they just ran them right into the ground," he says. "We saw an opportunity to make it a nicer place."

Be aware that many other conditions can affect the price of a laundry business as well. The cost of land in your area, high sewer connection fees and competition from other laundries all figure into the value.

If you're in a metropolitan area, you can compare the selling prices of similar laundromats, much like real estate agents do with houses. If a laundry that's the same size as the one you're looking at sells for $150,000 in a comparable neighborhood, you can expect to pay about that amount.

However, because the value of a laundromat depends on so many factors—lease, location, equipment and demographics, to name a few—it's best to seek advice from someone who has experience. A consultant or another laundry owner who's been in the business for a while can help you, as can a distributor. Just make sure the person you're seeking advice from is not going to profit from the sale.

Laundry consultant Lionel Bogut says that he once reviewed a laundromat with an asking price of $500,000. The potential buyers asked him to determine whether that was a fair price. He looked over the profits and expenses, the state of the equipment, and the conditions of the lease, and decided that the laundry was worth between $200,000 and $220,000. Eventually, the owner dropped the price. Says Bogut, "The [buyers] saved themselves a lot of money."

The New
Laundromat

So you like the idea of opening a laundry. It suits your working style and personality, and you understand the steps you need to take to research the market. The next step—and it's a crucial one—is to crunch the numbers. Before you plunge headfirst into the laundromat business, you must know how much cash you will need upfront and how much you can expect to make.

In this chapter we'll give you a rough idea of start-up costs and how to find the money to finance your business. Later, in Chapter 11, we'll walk you through the process of figuring out your projected net income.

Start-Up Costs

You can expect to encounter a number of basic start-up costs to get into the laundry business. Depending on whether you build a new laundry in a leased space or buy an existing one, your costs may include:

- Market research (literature/subscriptions/association fees)
- The cost of an existing laundry business
- Construction or remodeling (if you are building a new laundromat)
- Washer hook-up fees (sewer connection)
- Licenses/permits
- Equipment (See the "Equipment Basics Checklist" on page 50.)

Keep in mind that if you buy a laundry, you don't pay for licenses or sewer connection fees (unless you decide to have additional washers installed). But you will have to pay for renovation and any new equipment you decide to install if you want to update the laundry.

In addition to these basic start-up costs, you may also have a number of ongoing expenses—a subject we will return to in Chapter 11. These include:

- Lease/rental costs
- Utilities (gas, sewer, water and electric)
- Insurance (fire, theft and liability)
- Employee payroll/benefits
- Miscellaneous supplies (cleaning supplies, soap, invoices for wash-and-fold, bathroom supplies, etc.)

Research and Development

If you're new to the laundry business, you will need to spend some time getting to know it better. That includes reading everything you can on the subject, including current publications as well as previous issues of trade magazines and newsletters. It will also be important for you to join professional associations and to interview experienced laundry owners. While we can't put a figure on the time you'll spend conducting research, you can count on spending about $300 to $400 for literature and association fees.

Once you've completed your research, you will need to figure out how much it will cost to build your store—to remodel a space and fill it with laundry equipment—or to buy

Getting Off the Ground

Industry experts say a laundry takes between six months and a year to start turning a profit. "After that, you grow," says laundry consultant Lionel Bogut. "And you continue to grow as long as you take care of your customers and your equipment."

Collette Clarkson, who owns a laundry in Evans, Colorado, says she and her partner, Kim Clarkson, were "out of the red" in three months, and their business is still growing. On the other hand, Dave and Kris Anderson, with a laundromat in New Glarus, Wisconsin, have been in business for six years and are still breaking even. "Our goal is to get the equipment paid for as fast as we can," Dave says. His costs are a little higher than many other laundry owners because he purchased the property his store is located on.

an existing laundry. Whether you decide to buy or build, you can expect to pay between $200,000 and $500,000 for an average-size laundromat (about 2,000 square feet).

If you're buying an existing laundry, figuring out your major start-up costs is simple—just determine the value of the business. (See Chapter 4 to learn more about arriving at a fair price for a laundry.) If you plan to renovate the existing store by painting the interior or putting in new flooring, be sure to add these costs to your start-up expenses.

Figuring out your start-up costs involves a little more work if you decide to build. Since you'll be leasing a space that was something other than a laundry in a previous life, the cost of the construction is going to depend on how much remodeling you have to do. If the space you've chosen was formerly a beauty salon, for example, you're going to have to add enough water, sewer and gas pipes for the conversion to a laundry. You'll also have to provide enough electrical outlets, possibly move a few walls, and completely redecorate before it will look like a laundromat. You should hire a contractor to help you do all this remodeling (we'll return to this subject in Chapter 6).

In general, you can expect to pay about $200,000 in construction costs to remodel an average-size space (2,000 square feet). This includes the cost of installing your equipment and putting in folding tables and seating. The remainder of your major start-up costs will be buying the equipment itself.

Be aware that your construction costs can fluctuate due to factors like the one that Brian De Coster, a laundry owner in Iowa City, Iowa, describes. When he was negotiating a lease for his laundry, he tried to get a spot on the end of a strip mall. He failed: He lost it to a woman who wanted to open a deli. So his contractor had to figure out a way to duct the dryers out the back and up into the ceiling. If he'd had the end spot, the ducts could have been placed out the side instead, and he could have saved on construction costs.

Licenses and Hidden Fees

The licenses and permits you will need depend entirely on your location. Check with your municipality regarding:

- Business license
- Health department license (if you are serving food)
- Fire department permit
- Air and water pollution control permit
- Sign permit
- Public improvement fees
- Impact fees

Smart Tip

The SBA has a web site with links to states' licenses and permits web pages (not all states have such a web page). Check it out at www. sba.gov/hotlist/license.html.

You should also be aware of a few lesser-known fees that will affect you as a laundry owner. In many areas around the country, municipal water districts charge sewer connection fees. These can cost you anywhere from $200 to $8,000 per washer. If the fees are $8,000 per washer, the owner of a laundry with 30 washers must pay $240,000 in hook-up fees—almost what he'll pay for construction! Brian Wallace, president and CEO of the Coin Laundry Association, tells us that high hook-up fees are one of the biggest problems facing the coin laundry industry today. "Before you get too far down the road, make sure you understand what if any impact fees, tap-on fees, wastewater fees—they call them lots of things—there are," says Wallace. These fees are a major challenge to laundry developers. And in areas where operators are forced to pay these fees, the price of laundromats has also risen dramatically. If the fees are high in your chosen area, you may need to reconsider your entire plan.

In addition to sewer connection fees, you may find that you have to pay sewer and waste water fees, too—check with the local municipality. Don't neglect to check on these charges when you're researching a laundry business. After all, you will be using these utilities heavily, so you'll want to know if the monthly charges will be manageable from the get-go.

The Goods

If you decide to buy a laundry, you will already have a full complement of equipment—unless you want to replace a few of the older machines or add a few more machines to meet customer demand. However, if you

Dollar Stretcher

Your manufacturer may try to sell you a warranty, but distributor and Coin Laundry Association chairman Bob Eisenberg says don't waste your money: "Typically, for the first two or three years you aren't going to experience any problems."

decide to build a laundry, buying equipment will eat up virtually all the rest of your start-up costs. You can expect to pay between $150,000 and $300,000 to fill an average-size laundromat with washers and dryers. Refer to the "Equipment Basics Checklist" on page 50 as you read through our rundown of equipment you should buy for your new laundry.

Top-load washers cost between $500 and $700 each, and front-load washers cost between $3,500 and $20,000 each, depending on their size. One stacked dryer (which means two dryers arranged one on top of the other in a joined cabinet casing) costs between $5,000 and $6,000.

Smart Tip

The Coin Laundry Association offers tours of laundromats. This is a great opportunity for prospective laundry owners to see how different laundries are set up and run. Tour participants also have a chance to talk with successful owners. See the Appendix for information on how to contact the Coin Laundry Association.

If you want to add a card system, it will cost you in the neighborhood of $40,000 to $80,000, including readers on the machines, a card dispenser and cards, and the software to compute equipment usage and let you change prices. It's pricey, but take heart: With a card system, you don't have to buy a change machine, which runs in the ballpark of $1,000 to $3,000. For more information on card systems, see Chapter 7.

A water heating system will run you between $15,000 and $40,000, and a soap vending machine will cost between $500 and $1,500. Those laundry carts that let customers transport their clothes from washer to dryer cost $50 to $75 each. Supplies such as soap, cleaning equipment, signs, clocks, and trash cans should run another $750 to $1,000.

If you plan to offer wash-and-fold service, you will need a cash register, laundry scale, and counter where customers can pick up their laundry. A basic electronic cash register will run you about $300 to $3,000, depending on how fancy you want to get. A scale for weighing wash-and-fold laundry will cost you between $400 and $1,000. The cost of a counter should be covered under your construction/installation costs.

If you want to buy a snack or soda vending machine, it will cost you between $3,000 and $4,000. As an alternative, you could contract with a vending company: They pay for the machine and the snacks and sodas, and split the profits with you.

If you choose to add amenities, like TVs or computers for your customers to play on the internet, this will cost you, too. A TV will run you about $200 to $500, and a basic computer system will cost you in the neighborhood of $1,500 to $2,000. Also factor in monthly fees for an ISP, which will be around $40.

Finally, if you don't hire attendants, you might want to install a video security system. This will cost you between $6,000 and $10,000 or more, depending on the number of cameras and type of equipment you want. We said it would cost you.

▲

Other Equipment

You'll also need invoices to give to customers who drop off their laundry for wash-and-fold. You can buy basic invoices from an office supply store, or you can have special ones printed up with your store's name and policies.

If your laundry will be attended, you'll want a phone in the store. It should have an answering machine or a voice mail service. You're looking at paying $40 to $150 for a basic two-line speakerphone with auto-redial, memory and a mute button. To install a phone line in your store, it will cost you approximately $40 to $60. Expect to pay another $15 to $65 for an answering machine—or get voice mail for just $12 to $18 per month.

Consider buying a cell phone or pager if you'll be away from your laundry much of the time and your attendants or customers will need to reach you quickly. If you will have an unattended laundry without a phone and you plan to take care of your office work at home, you may want to consider installing a separate business line so you can be listed in the Yellow Pages.

Like any other small-business owner, you'll need equipment to run administrative tasks—paying bills, managing finances, calling repair people. A computer is not

---

Equipment Basics Checklist

Store Essentials
- ❏ Washers
- ❏ Dryers
- ❏ Water heating system
- ❏ Soap vending machine
- ❏ Change machines
- ❏ Laundry carts
- ❏ Folding tables
- ❏ Seats
- ❏ Miscellaneous supplies (soap, cleaning supplies, signs, clock, trash cans, bathroom supplies)

For Wash-and-Fold
- ❏ Counter
- ❏ Cash register
- ❏ Scale (for weighing laundry)
- ❏ Invoices

Office Supplies
- ❏ Computer
- ❏ Software
- ❏ Phone with answering machine
- ❏ Calculator
- ❏ Business stationery/cards

Optional Items
- ❏ Automatic lock system
- ❏ Timer for lights
- ❏ TVs/computers
- ❏ Snack or soda vending machines
- ❏ Video security system

essential, although it will make charting equipment use and keeping track of finances much easier. If you don't already have one, you can purchase a basic setup for $1,500 to $2,000, including a hard drive, monitor, modem and printer. A spreadsheet program such as Microsoft Excel or accounting software like Intuit QuickBooks will save you a lot of time. Expect to pay in the range of $100 to $400 for one of these programs.

You will probably need to copy a few documents and fax a few letters, but it's not likely to happen often enough to justify purchasing a copier or a fax machine. You will, however, need a good calculator for figuring out your income and expenses; this will cost anywhere from $5 to $50, depending on the model you decide to go with.

Business stationery is not essential, as you won't be writing letters to prospective clients, but it's convenient for writing letters to suppliers or repair companies. And you may want to buy business cards that you can pass out to prospective customers.

For Example . . .

On page 52, we've provided sample start-up costs for two hypothetical companies: Suds-R-Us, a large laundry with attendants and wash-and-fold service, and Squeaky Clean Wash-and-Dry, a smaller laundry with no attendants and fewer amenities.

The owner of Suds-R-Us built his new laundry in a 3,000-square-foot space that he rented in a strip mall. The construction costs associated with remodeling the space and converting it to a laundry cost him $300,000. He bought the following equipment and had it installed: 10 top-load washers, 10 18-pound front-load washers, five 30-pound front-loaders, five 50-pound front-loaders, one 75-pound front-loader, and 16 stacked dryers (32 dryers total). Including the water heating system, a card system that includes software, and a soap vending machine, his equipment cost him a total of $290,500. On top of this, the local utility district charges $500 to hook up each washer, so the owner had to pay a total of $15,500 to have all 31 washing machines hooked up.

Suds-R-Us has three employees and offers customers wash-and-fold service (with the associated costs of a cash register and laundry scale). Three TVs have also been provided for the customers, at a total cost of $900. While the owner decided to buy his own soap vending machine (for $1,500), he decided to cut costs by contracting with an outside company for soda and snack vending services. To advertise his new store, the owner took out ads in both the local newspaper and the Yellow Pages. He also organized a large grand opening to introduce his business to the neighborhood, and he sent a direct mail advertisement with a discount coupon to potential customers in the area.

The owners of Squeaky Clean, on the other hand, bought an existing laundry located in the business district of a small town. The owners decided to renovate the 1,000-square-foot store. They wanted to repaint, replace flooring, install some better

Start-Up Costs

Compare these start-up costs for our two hypothetical businesses: the newly built Suds-R-Us and Squeaky Clean, an existing laundry that the owner bought and renovated.

Start-Up Expenses	Suds-R-Us	Squeaky Clean
Cost of existing laundry business	$0	$150,000
Construction/remodeling (new laundry)	$300,000	$0
Renovations (to existing laundry)	$0	$25,000
Dues and literature	$400	$400
Washer hook-up fees (sewer connection)	$15,500	$400
Business licenses/permits	$100	$0
Advertising/grand opening	$6,000	$500
Top-loaders ($600 each)	$6,000	$0
18-pound front-loaders ($3,500 each)	$35,000	$0
30-pound front-loaders ($5,000 each)	$25,000	$5,000
50-pound front-loaders ($9,000 each)	$45,000	$9,000
75-pound front-loaders	$13,000	$0
Stacked dryers ($5,000 each)	$80,000	$5,000
Card system	$60,000	$0
Water heating system	$25,000	$0
Soap dispenser	$1,500	$0
Laundry carts ($75 each)	$750	$0
Laundry scale	$750	$0
Cash register	$600	$0
Change machine	$0	$0
Office equipment	$250	$100
Phone installation	$50	$0
Televisions ($300 each)	$900	$300
Video security system	$0	$6,000
Miscellaneous supplies	$1,000	$400
Total Start-Up Costs	**$616,800**	**$202,100**

lighting, and add several new machines to meet customer demand. The renovations came to $25,000, and the new equipment cost another $19,000.

The business came with 5-year-old equipment, including 10 top-loaders, three 30-pound front-loaders, five stacked dryers (10 dryers), a change machine, and a soap vending machine. The owners decided to buy and install an additional 30-pound front-loader and one 50-pound front-loader. They had to pay $200 in hook-up fees per washer. They also had one stacked dryer (two dryers) installed to accommodate the additional volume of clothes from the front-loaders.

The owners of Squeaky Clean decided to put a TV set in their store for customers to watch while waiting for their laundry. And since they did not want to hire attendants, the owners installed a video security system for safety purposes. Squeaky Clean machines take coins, and, like Suds-R-Us, the vending services are contracted. To announce that the store is under new management, the owners decided to organize a small grand opening celebration. They also placed a Yellow Pages ad.

Finding the Money

OK, you're looking at spending hundreds of thousands of dollars to buy or build a laundry. Where are you going to get all this money? Wherever you can.

"Financing is a major issue of the coin laundry industry," says CPA and laundry consultant Richard Weisinger. "Lenders want something that holds its value as collateral. Laundromat equipment is a heavily wasting asset. It wears out very quickly, and bankers are loathe to lend into an industry where the bulk of the value of the industry is tied up in intangibles [such as customer loyalty]."

That doesn't mean, however, that banks won't make loans to laundry entrepreneurs. Weisinger adds that if you have been in business before and have a good credit history, you should be able to get a loan. Most of the entrepreneurs interviewed for this book received loans from their local banks. A few also used family money. Those who had relationships with people at their banks approached them and received good deals.

Distributors, the folks who'll sell you your equipment, will also help you finance a laundry. Many times, if a prospective owner can't get a loan from a bank, the equipment manufacturer, through the distributor, will finance a store. Paul Donovan, former vice president of sales and marketing at laundry equipment

> **Bright Idea**
> Consider getting a revolving line of credit from your bank, a sort of preapproved loan that lets you borrow money quickly whenever you need it. If you have a major equipment failure or fire, for example, you can get money immediately to fix the problem.

▲

distributor PWS, says that PWS helps out entrepreneurs who show good business smarts.

Distributors want to see a business plan, including whether the store will be attended, what sort of services will be offered, and what kind of equipment will be promoted. "If someone comes out and says 'Here I am; I'm 26 years old, and I want to finance at 90 percent, and I've never run a business,' then we're going to be a little tougher on them," Donovan says.

Weisinger warns that distributors often offer sandwich financing, meaning that they borrow from the bank to loan to entrepreneurs and mark up the rate. The entrepreneurs interviewed for this book said that they received a better deal from banks. "The distributor couldn't even come close," says Collette Clarkson, who runs a laundry in Evans, Colorado.

Choosing a Structure

Before you approach a lender, you should decide what sort of business structure you want to choose for your laundry. You can operate as a sole proprietor, a corporation, or a cross between these two business structures—meaning a limited liability company, an S corporation, or a partnership.

Operating as a sole proprietor is the simplest way to go—you just add a form to your personal income tax. You can use business losses to offset your personal income, thereby reducing your taxes. This is especially helpful in the first year of business, before your laundry has reached full swing. The downside is that you're personally liable in case someone falls in your laundry and sues.

At the other extreme, operating as a corporation protects your personal assets from business debts, but you can't use business losses to reduce your personal income tax. And incorporating your business is much more complicated and expensive.

The rest of the business structures you can choose from offer some sort of compromise between a sole proprietorship and a corporation.

Weisinger often recommends operating as an S corporation, but he says that a particular business structure is not crucial for laundromats. "There's no one answer," he says. "It'll depend on your exposure, the simplicity in your life. The moment you form a corporation or a limited liability company, you have just bought yourself another tax preparation fee." He also notes that while operating as a sole proprietorship makes you personally liable in case a customer sues, your insurance will pay for that.

Calling in
the Experts

You may have decided to start a laundry business because you like the idea of working on your own. But you can't do it all by yourself. You'll need lots of help from experts —from equipment distributors and accountants to repairpersons—to get off to a good start. In this chapter, we'll describe what these and other experts can do to help you get your laundry up and running. We'll also cover how to select good ones to work with.

Distributors

Distributors are the folks who sell you laundry equipment. Everyone who opens a new laundromat, or renovates an existing one, will need to work with a distributor before he or she can open. Even those who buy laundromats in pristine condition will eventually call on a distributor to replace worn out washers and dryers. Distributors work regionally, and they sell equipment from certain manufacturers. So while Joe Distributor sells only Wash King brand equipment in southern Florida, for example, Jane Distributor sells only Super Suds brand equipment, and only in Montana.

These people do much more than sell equipment, however. They can advise you on almost any aspect of your laundry. Distributors will advise you first of all on your location. To determine whether the site will be successful, they will evaluate the customer base surrounding the site, as well as parking and visibility. They'll also look at whether you have enough space for the necessary equipment and whether the site can be remodeled to accommodate a laundry.

Brian De Coster, a laundry owner in Iowa City, Iowa, already knew a distributor through his rental business. When he decided to open a laundromat, he asked the distributor about several locations he had found. The distributor nixed them all. "The guy said it wasn't going to work because of lack of parking," De Coster says. Finally, he found a location his distributor did like. He built his laundry there, and business has taken off—in fact, he now owns four laundries.

Distributors will also help you with your equipment mix. They can tell you how many of each type of machine you'll need, based on the customers in your location. (We'll talk more about equipment mix in Chapter 7.) They'll also install the equipment and offer you training in maintaining and repairing it. Distributors act as brokers in buying and selling a store, too.

"The distributor is really the local expert," says Brian Wallace, president and CEO of the Coin Laundry Association. Distributors earn their money by selling you equipment; they won't charge you for giving advice or for the time they spend explaining the business to you.

Choosing a Distributor

To find a distributor in your area, talk with other laundry owners, preferably ones who won't be in direct competition with you. Ask them whether the distributor they used was helpful, knowledgeable and honest about potential problems. You want a

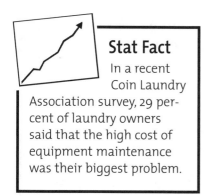

distributor who will steer you away from bad locations—like the one that helped De Coster.

Also contact your local coin laundry association. These organizations have collective knowledge about distributors in your area and should be able to refer you to someone. Take the time to interview any distributors who have been recommended to you. You'll be working with your distributor very closely for a while, so you want to find someone with whom you feel comfortable. Make sure he or she is responsive to questions, personable, and easy to talk with.

"I highly recommend that people who get into the business interview multiple distributors," says Wallace. Although each distributor sells only one or maybe two makes of equipment, Wallace and other experts recommend that new laundry owners choose a person rather than a machine. The various brands of washers and dryers being manufactured now are all top quality, they say. What will really make a difference in your business is a good distributor who can advise you well.

"It's really more important who you buy from than what you buy," Wallace says. "You'd much rather find a distributor who's knowledgeable of the industry, or that particular market, and use whatever brand of equipment they happen to carry."

"I agree completely," says Paul Partyka of *American Coin-Op* magazine. "Go with the distributor rather than the equipment." He says that a few people have preferences for certain brands but adds that all brands seem to perform well. "I think people are generally satisfied with their equipment."

A Second Opinion

Wise distributors know that they will do well in the long run if they advise you honestly and help you avoid pitfalls. If your store is successful, you'll likely want to open another one. Or you will recommend them to new owners.

But not all distributors are wise. And keep in mind that your distributor is in the business to sell you equipment. Distributors don't make any money unless you buy or build a store. "[Distributors] are the worst possible people to go to to get an unbiased opinion," says Richard Weisinger, a laundry consultant. "That has nothing to do with their integrity or lack of it. It is simply how they earn their living—by selling stores."

When you're buying a laundry, or building a new one, you're paying hundreds of thousands of dollars, so it's smart to play it safe. Get a second opinion. Even if you'd trust your distributor with your kids on a white-water rafting trip in the middle of winter, it's still a good idea to get someone else's viewpoint. The second opinion could come from another distributor, experienced laundry owners, your laundry association, or a consultant.

Consultants

There's a small group of people, most of them former laundry owners, who act as consultants for the laundry industry. You pay them by the hour, so they have no interest in whether you buy equipment or a particular store, or whether you even get into the laundry business.

Consultants will tell you if they think your location is good, whether your equipment mix is correct, whether the rent is fair, and what sort of profit you can expect from a certain store. They may even be able to estimate how many turns per day you can expect (how many times each piece of equipment will be used each day). This estimate will help you to price your services correctly.

They can inspect a store and tell you what sort of shape the equipment is in; they can also tell you if there are any problems with the building itself. Consultants can advise you on how to run a wash-and-fold service and how to supervise your employees. Most importantly, they can determine how much a store is worth. In short, a consultant can advise you on just about every aspect of your business. They will cost you, though. Consultants charge from $150 to $300 per hour. For a listing of several laundry consultants, take a look at the Appendix in the back of the book.

Bright Idea

After your laundry has been up and running for a while, ask a consultant to come and evaluate it for you to see where you could be making more money. There's bound to be something you can do to cut costs or bring in more customers.

Dollar Stretcher

If you want to use a consultant, gather beforehand all the information about the laundry you want to purchase—demographics, a copy of the lease, information on fees and permits, utility bills, expense and income reports from the current owner, a pro forma from a distributor, and warranties. That way, you save yourself the hourly cost of having the consultant do this preliminary research.

Contractors

Whether you are building a new laundry or renovating an existing one, you'll need to hire a contractor (unless you are a contractor, like Dave Anderson, one of our entrepreneurs). There are a few contractors who specialize in laundries, but don't go too much out of your way to find one. Plumbing is plumbing, and tiling is tiling—whether it's for a house or for a laundromat.

"There really isn't that much difference between the construction of a laundry and any other kind of construction," says laundry consultant Lionel Bogut. "It's not that different from what it is in an average home. Just find an experienced, all-around good contractor."

Beware!

Make sure any contractor you hire is bonded. This means the contractor is insured, so you won't be liable in case of injury or accidents on the job. It also protects you in case the contractor destroys any equipment or creates any structural damage.

The best way to find a good contractor is to ask everyone you know—neighbors, business associates and friends—for recommendations. Contact those who are recommended to you and ask them to give you an estimate of how much it will cost to build or renovate your laundry. Don't just go with the cheapest one—you don't want anyone to cut corners. Try to find a happy medium between price and quality. And before you hire your contractor, be sure to verify that he or she is properly licensed.

Designers

You may also want to work with a designer or architect when building or renovating your laundry. Most of the entrepreneurs interviewed for this book just designed their stores with the help of their distributors, but a few did choose to hire professional designers.

De Coster, who wanted a bold image for his store, gathered photographs of laundromats he liked and took them to a designer. The two of them worked together to create a store that made them both happy. With its bright colors and bold signs, De Coster says his store has the kind of look he wants—fresh and new.

Repairpersons

If you have new equipment, for the first few years you won't have to worry much about repairs. After that, however, you can expect machines to start giving you trouble. So, unless you're very handy and expect to fix the machines in your store by yourself, you will likely need a repairperson. Don't wait until a machine breaks to find one, though. It's much better to have a repairperson lined up beforehand. If you have a regular repairperson, you can get your machines fixed quickly and efficiently by someone you know is competent.

Tim O'Connell, who owns 24 stores around Syracuse, New York, has two full-time mechanics. "They go as needed," he said. "The attendants call when there's something wrong." Of course, a full-time repairperson makes sense only if you have a number of stores.

To find a repairperson, check with other laundry owners in your area. You may also be able to use a repair service offered by your equipment manufacturer; ask your dis-

Association Expertise

Professional associations can provide invaluable help to new business owners. The staff and members are usually very experienced and knowledgeable about their industry, and they're eager to provide an unbiased opinion (as long as you're a member).

There is only one national laundry association, the Coin Laundry Association (it covers card-operated laundries, too); it has several affiliate organizations around the country. There are also separate regional associations—ask laundry owners in your area where you can find these groups.

Associations hold meetings and other networking opportunities and often publish guidebooks and newsletters, which they issue at a discount for members. Annual dues for associations usually run from $150 to $250. The Coin Laundry Association has a hotline for its members. If you're unsure about any aspect of your business—whether it's location, the right equipment mix or anything else—you can call during business hours and ask the opinion of an expert.

tributor about going this route. In general, you can expect to pay repairpersons between $250 and $350 a week, depending on the size of your laundry.

Other Expertise

When you're setting up your business, you should also hire the services of an attorney or an accountant. These professionals will help you decide on an appropriate business structure and make sure you're up on all the tax issues. As with hiring a repairperson, it's best to find a good lawyer or accountant before a crisis situation. How do you choose a good one? Rather than just flipping through the Yellow Pages, you should contact your local bar association for a referral. Another option is to ask other professionals you know, such as bankers or business owners in the laundry industry. You can network with other laundry owners through your local coin-laundry association and ask for their recommendations.

Getting
Equipped

Alaundromat is all about the equipment inside it. While good customer service will help attract repeat business to your store, having the right number of quality machines (all in good working order) is paramount to your success. This chapter will cover the basic laundry equipment you'll need for your store: washers, dryers, water heaters, change machines, folding tables, and laundry carts. We'll talk about the ideal equipment mix for your laundry and how to arrange equipment inside your store. We'll also look at the "coin *vs.* card" debate and find out why one system may be better than the other for your laundromat.

Machine Basics

Customers will visit a laundromat to use three types of machines: top-load washers, front-load washers, and dryers. The top-loaders are the standard washing machines you find in most homes—with a door that opens on top and an agitator in the middle. These can hold about 8 pounds of laundry.

Front-loaders are large washing machines with a door in the front and a drum that looks like that in a dryer. These come in various sizes, and people in the industry refer to them according to how much laundry the machines can hold, such as 25-pound front-loaders or 35-pounders. The smallest of these washers can hold 18 pounds of laundry, the largest as much as 125 pounds. Front-loaders use about half as much water as top-loaders per pound of wash: An 18-pound front-loader, for example, will use about the same amount of water as a top-loader. These machines are real moneymakers for laundry businesses because they're so efficient.

The dryers in laundromats are similar to dryers in homes, except that they are larger. They can hold two loads of laundry from a top-load washer. Most commercial dryers manufactured these days are stacked dryers, which means two dryers sit one on top of the other in a joined cabinet casing. If you have 20 stacked dryers in your store, you have a total of 40 dryers for customers to use.

The Right Mix

When you're setting up your laundry, you should think about what types of machines you want to install and how many of each you will need. The first thing to consider is whether you'll have the right ratio of washers to dryers. If you have too few dryers, for example, your customers will have to wait around before they can take their clothes out of the washer and put them in the dryer. This means that other customers won't be able to get their laundry started and may go to another laundry instead.

The rule of thumb in the industry is to have one dryer for every two top-load washers and one for each front-load washer. This rule is based on the fact that customers generally put two loads of laundry from top-load washing machines into one dryer. If they use the front-loaders, however, they generally place one load of laundry into one dryer. Since drying can take a little longer than washing, some experts recommend that you add a few extra dryers above this estimate. "If you have 40 top-loaders, you want 21 to 22 dryers," says consultant Lionel Bogut. With the right equipment mix, he says,

Speedy Spinner

Besides washers and dryers, there's another piece of equipment your customers can use: extractors. These are machines that spin at high speeds and take out much of the water left after the washer spin cycle. They can reduce drying time by as much as half.

Tom Leavitt has an extractor in one of his Seattle-area laundries. His customers like to use it for items that absorb a lot of water such as towels and bedspreads because it cuts down on the drying time. It's also useful for items such as drapes, rugs, or comforters that can't take a lot of heat. The extractor costs customers 69 cents per load to use.

your customers can flow through your laundry quickly, leaving room for the next customer. "You have to constantly look at turnover in the laundry," he says. "In many laundries you can increase business by taking out machines and putting in folding areas and dryers."

Next, you'll need to consider the number of top-loaders as compared with the number of front-loaders. Laundries in the United States have relied fairly heavily on top-loaders, but this practice is going the way of the dodo bird. Front-loaders last so much longer than top-loaders, and they save so much energy, that some distributors sell only front-loaders. "I don't put top-load washers in stores anymore," said Bob Eisenberg, a laundry owner and distributor with Qualclean Equipment in Philadelphia. Front-loaders are also a better deal for customers, as one of these machines can wash more than twice the amount of laundry that a top-load washer can—for less than twice the price. And customers, even those with washers at home, can use them to wash large items such as quilts and sleeping bags.

If you're near a college or senior residence, however, you may want to include some top-loaders. Most of these people will be single and won't have enough clothes every week to justify the large machines. Cindy Patel, owner of Mountain Wash Laundry in Shelby, North Carolina, included eight top-loaders in her 35-washer store. "The seniors like to wash their laundry in smaller loads," she said, "and women like to wash their undergarments separately." Also, some customers are used to top-loaders and intimidated by the front-loaders; if they don't see any top-loaders in your store, they may pass it up for the next laundry.

It's always a good idea to discuss equipment mix with your distributor. With his or her expertise, you should be able to determine the sort of mix that will suit your store best.

Where Everything Goes

If it's possible in your space, you want to place your washers and dryers opposite each other. For example, if your laundry is long and narrow, you want to put all the washers on one side and all the dryers on the other. Or if you have an island of machines intersecting the store, you could put all the washers against the walls and the dryers in the middle. This setup lets customers move their laundry quickly from one machine to the next, and it makes room for the next customer. See the "Sample Floor Plan" on page 67.

See the "Sample Floor Plan" on page 67.

Smart Tip

Tip...

To help customers get their clothes from the washers to the dryers, you should provide them with laundry carts they can wheel around. Owners of unattended laundries complain that these tend to disappear; however, you can buy carts with vertical bars that prevent customers from taking them out the door.

Machines that are placed opposite each other should be spaced at least four feet apart, though six feet is better. Make sure they're far enough apart that customers aren't bumping into each other.

Although some of your customers are going to shove their clothes right from the dryer into their duffel bags and set off for home, most of them are going to be a little more careful with their clothing. You'll need folding tables, counter-high tables that customers can use to fold their clothes, sheets, or towels before they take them home. Place the folding tables near the dryers so customers can dump their laundry directly from the dryers onto the tables. If you have folding tables placed opposite washers or dryers, allow at least four feet between the tables and the machines; you want your customers to have adequate space to transfer their laundry between the machines and from the dryers to the counters.

It's best to place your front-load washers as close to the entrance of the store as possible. Customers who come in with huge bags of laundry will want to unload them as soon as possible. Another reason for this placement is that customers are more likely to use front-loaders if those are the washing machines they see first. Remember: It's to your advantage to have customers use front-load washers, because these machines bring in more money than top-loaders while using less water per pound of laundry.

Equipment TLC

Once you've filled your store with all this great equipment, you need to do everything you can to keep it running smoothly. Any store can expect to have one or two machines out of order now and then, but you'll be losing a lot of money if more than that are on the fritz. Having machines in poor repair also sends a message to your customers that you don't care about your store—a message that won't encourage repeat business.

Dollar Stretcher

Purchase parts for your machines and supplies, such as toilet paper and cleaning fluids, in bulk. You'll not only get a discount, but you'll save on the time and money spent buying these goods.

So you'll want to repair machines as soon as they break. In addition, you may want to consider preventive maintenance to head off potential problems with older equipment. If you're not handy with machines, don't panic. You can hire a repairperson to do all the work for you (take a look back at Chapter 6 for a refresher). But if you can do some of the repair work yourself, you'll save money. You'll also get the machines up and running more quickly if you jump on the problem rather than wait for the repairperson to show up. Most of the entrepreneurs interviewed for this book knew next to nothing about laundry equipment when they started their businesses, yet they are doing many of the necessary repairs themselves.

"We're learning by trial and error," says The Last Load owner Collette Clarkson in Evans, Colorado. She and her partner, Kim Clarkson, attended a repair school offered by their distributor. They found it very helpful, she says, and would recommend it to new laundry owners.

In Hot Water

That little water heater in your home that runs out of hot water after three showers isn't going to cut it for your laundromat. You'll need a sophisticated water heating system that will provide enough hot water for everyone, quickly. Some systems circulate water continuously throughout the store so that even the washers farthest from the heater provide hot water as soon as customers need it.

You might also want to think about a heat recovery system for hot water. These systems save energy and cut utility bills—one of your biggest expenses. They work by running cold incoming water through coils that wrap around the waste water pipe. When hot water drains through the pipe, the water in the coils gets heated. This fresh, warm water then goes to the water heater where it will be heated up the rest of the way. Since less energy is needed to heat the warmed water, you will save on your monthly gas bill.

Some laundry owners are saving money by using several smaller water heaters instead of one large one. During slow times, only one heater is working, thereby saving the owner the cost of keeping a large amount of water heated at all times.

Determining which system is the best for your store will depend on the size of your laundry, the hours it's open, the price of utilities in your area, and other factors. Talk with your distributor and your contractor about choosing the right water heating system for your store.

The Card Advantage

As we have mentioned briefly already, manufacturers now build washers and dryers that take cards rather than coins. Card systems are a fairly recent development, though. Brian Wallace of the Coin Laundry Association estimates that only 500 to 1,000 of the 35,000 or so laundries in the country are card-operated.

In a laundry with a card system, customers purchase a card from a card machine, often making a deposit of a few dollars for the card. The rest of the money is stored on the card much like it is on a phone card. Customers then swipe the card through the machines they want to use, and the machines subtract the price. If a customer puts too much money on a card, you can refund the amount left on the card.

There are many advantages to having a card system in your laundry:

- With a card system, you can change prices at any time. You can raise prices by pennies rather than 25 cents.
- You can issue discount cards that take off less money with each swipe. You can offer a discount to your regular customers by giving $22 of equipment use for $20, for example. You can easily offer specials to students or seniors, or to customers who use the laundry during slow periods.

The Cashless Crowd

Just think how much your customers will appreciate your store if they don't have to lug their laundry to an ATM before they drag it into the laundromat. If you're planning on purchasing a card system, ask about a card machine that accepts debit and credit cards.

Bob Eisenberg installed such a machine at his store in Upper Darby, Pennsylvania, and says it has taken in $20,000 over five months. "It probably adds between 10 and 15 percent to my business," he says. These machines cost about $4,000 to $5,000.

Another way to draw customers who like the convenience of cards is to install an ATM. These machines cost about $6,000 to $8,000, and owners usually charge customers $1.50 to $2 to use them.

Eisenberg said he decided not to charge customers extra to use his credit-card-accepting machine. Even though it costs him 3.5 percent of each sale, he says, "I didn't want to get customers mad at me. I'd rather give the customer other benefits."

Sample Floor Plan

- You don't have to carry around bags of coins. This also means you don't have to count coins.
- You get paid in advance. A customer will put $20 or $30 on a card, then hold onto it until the following week.
- The card keeps customers coming back to your store. Since customers often add more value to their cards than they intend to use in one trip, you know they'll be returning to use up the balance.
- A card system's software will automatically compute for you which machines are being used and how often—which means less work for you.

> **Smart Tip** *Tip...*
>
> Your customer base may determine whether a card system will work for your store. Seniors are often more apprehensive about using cards, and tourists often don't want the trouble of buying a card and figuring out the system for just one or two visits.

Cindy Patel, who decided to go with a card system, says, "It's working great. I didn't see any people who, after I showed them how it worked, decide that they didn't want to use it."

Bob Eisenberg adds, "There's a whole laundry list of reasons" to use a card system. In his store, Family Wash Day in Upper Darby, Pennsylvania, he offers a discount on Tuesdays that is easy to implement, thanks to the card system, which can be programmed to charge a lower amount on a given day. "That has turned my slowest day into my busiest day," he says. "My software just takes care of it and automatically changes the price at 12:01 A.M. No one has to do anything."

Eisenberg adds that the card system is a benefit for customers, too: "I have 75-pound washers in my store that I vend for $7.45. How much time does it take to put in 30 quarters?"

Keep the following guidelines in mind when making a decision between a card system and the traditional coin system. A card system may be the best choice for your store if:

- You have the money to purchase the system.
- Your customers tend to be regulars.
- You want to give discounts and specials to certain groups.
- You don't want to carry around bags of coins.
- Noncustomers keep using your change machines for bus or parking fares.

Happy with Coins

Not everyone is sold on card systems. Several of the entrepreneurs interviewed for this book decided against cards when they built their stores. They didn't want to pay the

Smart Tip

If you have an unattended laundry, always have two working coin changers. If one machine breaks or runs out of coins, customers can use the other one, and you'll keep them in your store.

extra $40,000 to $80,000 for the system, and they felt customers would be more comfortable with coins.

Collette Clarkson says she and her partner considered cards but decided against them after talking with other laundry owners. "With quarters, it's something people always have," she says. "They don't like having to buy the card. They like having the freedom to come and go as they please, and go where they want."

Dave Anderson of Alpine Laundry also decided against a card system. Dave built his New Glarus, Wisconsin, laundry next to a coin-operated car wash, so he figured customers from the car wash would be more likely to use his laundry if it were coin-operated as well. Another consideration for Anderson was the fact that New Glarus is a tourist town, so much of his business consists of one-time-only customers. He felt that customers wouldn't want to go to the trouble of buying a card. Even if they did, he has an unattended laundry and wouldn't be able to give refunds to anyone with value left on a card at the end of their vacation. "[My distributor] felt with the tourist trade that it made more sense," says Anderson. And he feels it was the right decision: "I've never heard anyone complain about our coin system."

If you go with coins over cards, you must have change machines in your store. Change machines are the lifeblood of any coin-operated laundry. If customers can't make change, they can't use your machines, and you'll be out of business in a hurry. You may want to have two, just in case one breaks. Place both near the front window to discourage theft and always be sure they're in good working condition.

As you weigh the pros and cons of going with a coin system, see if the factors listed below apply to you. Coins may be a better choice for your laundry if:

- You don't want to pay for an expensive card system.
- Many of your customers are vacationers or infrequent users who are not likely to buy cards.
- Your customers speak different languages, and you won't be able to explain the system to everyone.
- You don't have an attendant to help customers use the system and give customers refunds.

Beware!

To discourage counterfeiters, the U.S. Mint issues new bills and coins every few years. Older coin changers may not be able to read the new bills. When you're purchasing a changer (or a store with a changer), make sure it can accept the newest bills from the Mint. Some changers also come with low-cost or free upgrades.

8

Dressing
the Store

If you're building a laundromat, you'll need to do more to your store than just load it with equipment—you'll need to design and decorate it. If you're buying an existing laundromat, you'll likely want to update its appearance. A well-decorated store isn't just pleasing to the eye. As we've said before, the laundry industry is a mature industry, so you'll need to use everything in your arsenal to win customers from your competitors.

You'll want to start with a store that looks good and feels comfortable; after all, you need to provide customers with a more pleasant atmosphere than your competition offers. A little entertainment for adults and children alike goes a long way toward winning customers. Brainwash, a popular laundry in San Francisco, includes a full-service café. Customers can dump a load of clothes, then go have a meal or a cup of joe while they're waiting. Others have tanning salons, cafes, or even mailboxes for rent. This chapter will cover decorating and amenities—the fine touches that will keep your customers returning.

General Guidelines

When it comes to putting in the major components of your store's interior—flooring, windows, lighting and signs—first of all, think clean. We're back to that familiar refrain: Customers want to visit a clean store. They'll be visiting your laundry to get clothes clean, not to dirty them in dryers that have mysterious substances stuck inside or on folding tables that haven't been wiped down. Anything you can do to enhance the cleanliness of your store will reassure customers.

Besides, it's much more pleasant to hang around in a nice-looking store—your customers have to stay there for a couple of hours, so give them something enjoyable to look at. They don't want to stay in a store with peeling paint, burned-out light bulbs, and cracked ceiling tiles. By keeping your store looking nice, you give customers the message that you care about them and want their business.

Here are some general pointers for decorating your laundry:

- *Go for a modern appearance.* If your store looks like it hasn't been touched since 1965, customers will wonder not only about its cleanliness but whether the equipment works.

- *Use lighter colors for walls, ceilings and floors.* These areas reflect light; as a result, your store will appear brighter if you use lighter colors. With reflected light, you may also spend less on electricity.

- *Keep the design of the store as open as possible.* You don't want any hidden spaces where thieves can lurk.

- *Use adequate lighting.* Customers want to see their clothes clearly, and they want to feel safe.

Floor It

Choosing flooring for your store will be one of your most important decorating decisions. The first thing customers will notice is the floor, so you want to make a strong statement. Collette Clarkson, an Evans, Colorado, laundry owner,

> **Beware!**
> Don't place too many signs in your windows. For safety reasons, you want to keep those panes of glass as open as possible.

> **Bright Idea**
>
> Place your coin changers near the front window of your laundromat so people on the street can see them. Also make sure they're well lit. Thieves are less likely to try to break into change machines when they have an audience.

says she and her partner chose white floor tiles for their store because they felt that white looked cleaner than any other color.

Since you or your employees will be mopping the floor every day, you want your flooring to be easy to clean, too. Tiles and certain types of linoleum are best; carpeting is not. Dave and Kris Anderson chose carpeting for their New Glarus, Wisconsin, store, a decision they now regret. While carpeting is comfortable for his customers to stand on, he and his wife, Kris, find it too difficult to clean. They have to vacuum it daily and shampoo it frequently. "That was one thing we wish we hadn't done," Kris says.

Keep in mind that you want a floor that's skidproof. If a washer leaks or a customer spills some water, you don't want all your employees and customers sliding and crashing onto the floor.

Finally, you want a floor that will be as resistant as possible to water damage. Check with your contractor about good quality flooring that offers durability, traction and a surface that's easy to clean.

Window Dressing

Be sure to front your store with large, plate-glass windows. Windows showcase your laundromat, which may attract customers who decide they like the look of your store. They also give customers a sense of security, since passersby can easily see what's happening inside the store. And large windows let you capture natural light, saving electricity and providing a more comfortable atmosphere.

Sign Away

You'll need signs inside your laundry, both to inform customers about your policies and to protect yourself against liability. Don't hand-write your signs: Spend the money to have some printed. This tells your customers that you're a professional laundry owner who cares about your store's appearance.

When coming up with the text for your signs, avoid the "No" syndrome—as in "No Smoking," "No Sitting on Equipment," "No Loitering," "No Eating," etc. No one likes being lectured to, so at least try to use the word "please." You'll find customers more willing to follow your rules if you speak to them nicely. Also try to give them alternatives:

> **Bright Idea**
>
> If you have a video game machine in your store, be sure to keep the screen clean. Customers are more likely to play games when they can see them clearly.

From Palm Trees to Planets

If you choose to incorporate a theme in the décor of your laundry, here are some ideas to get you started:

○ *The Old West.* You could have cowboy music on the radio, westerns on the TV, Texas landscapes on the walls, and a rocking horse for the children.

○ *The Tropics.* Your store could be transformed with palm trees (real or fake), Hawaiian shirts on the walls, and surf tunes on the radio.

○ *Outer Space.* You could run science fiction movies on the TV, have a rocket model that kids can play on, and paint the walls with stars and planets.

For example, "Please don't smoke inside the store. We have a bench outside for those of you who smoke."

Be sure to place signs saying that you are not responsible for theft or damage. This will help you in case of lawsuits. Finally, put up signs in all the languages your customers speak. If your laundry is in a neighborhood populated with Vietnamese immigrants, for example, get help from someone who speaks the language, or hire a translator to write signs in Vietnamese. Those potential customers who don't speak English will feel welcome at your store.

Setting Yourself Apart

Consider giving your store a theme or a gimmick. For example, one store in San Francisco plays classic black-and-white movies on their TV, and the walls are covered with photographs of movie stars from the 1920s and 1930s. Another store in Texas displays the owner's collection of antique laundry equipment. Iowa City, Iowa, laundry owner Brian De Coster chose humor: He plays comedy channels on his TVs and places signs with clever puns, such as "We have a dryer sense of humor" and "We never clothes." (His store is open 24 hours.)

A theme gives your store more personality; customers will remember it, and they'll find your laundry a more interesting place to come to. A clever gimmick may also get you some free publicity from the local press. If you want to create a gimmick for your laundromat, think about who your customers are and what sort of theme they will appreciate. One owner in Southern California, with customers from all over Latin America, hung his laundry with flags from several of his customers' native homelands and started serving traditional Latin American food.

Beware!

Don't forget to look at your laundromat from a toddler's point of view. Get down on your hands and knees, and crawl all around your store looking for potential hazards. You'll likely see some things you've never noticed before that might be relatively easy to fix.

For the Little Kids

Many laundry owners are realizing that they can increase business by providing a play area for children. Often, customers need to bring their children to the laundromat, so giving little ones something to do makes the laundry chore much easier on parents. Having an area set aside for children can also help keep them from running around and possibly getting hurt or damaging equipment.

Collette Clarkson and her partner have a play area for children. They have a TV with a VCR, children's videos and toys. "We wind up picking up a lot of toys," she says, "but they love it."

If you want to put in an area specifically for children, check with your insurance agent and your city or county officials regarding liability issues. These professionals should be able to tell you how to design the area to maximize safety and make sure you won't be responsible in case a child gets hurt. In fact, you may need to place signs saying you're not responsible for children's safety.

For the Big Kids

Even adults will get bored at a laundromat. After all, mostly what they are doing is waiting around for clothes to wash and dry. Many laundries these days have one or more TVs mounted to the wall. Some laundries keep the TVs tuned to one channel, some play videos, and others let customers change the channels themselves.

If your laundry is unattended and you want to let customers change the channel, mount the TV low enough on the wall so they can reach the channel and volume buttons. Customers are likely to walk off with a remote control, even if it's tacked to a table.

Brian De Coster put in phone jacks near a table so customers can plug in their laptops. He placed a sign above the table saying "Internet Access" to let customers know about the service. "People have expressed that they really appreciate it," he says. To ensure people don't walk in with a phone and call Finland or Saudi Arabia, De Coster has put toll restrictions on the lines.

Many laundry owners also have pinball and video games for their customers. Clarkson says a video game vendor approached her about having a videogame console in her store. He put a machine in at no cost to her, and they split the profits 50–50. "We've seen as much as $300 a month off the video game," Clarkson says. They change the game every so often to keep customers from getting bored.

You can talk to your distributor to find vendors that specialize in game machines, or check the Yellow Pages under "Games" or "Video Games."

▲

To Smoke or Not to Smoke

The smoking decision may not be up to you. Some cities and states are passing laws banning smoking in all public areas, including laundromats. But if you do have a choice, here are a few things to consider.

Laundry owners who have decided to ban smoking in their stores say their customers (even the smokers) appreciate cleaner-smelling clothing. And the non-smokers like the cleaner air. Other laundry owners say their smoking customers don't like having to stand outside, especially in foul weather, or having to wait until their wash is done to light up.

If you decide to ban smoking, place signs around your store reminding customers not to smoke. Try making humorous ones, such as "You light up my day—just don't light up in the laundry. Please refrain from smoking." Jokes help soften the blow to those customers dying for a nicotine fix. You or your attendants may have to remind smokers for the first few months after you open or after you decide to go smoke-free.

And if you are going to ask customers to smoke outside, be sure to place a container for cigarette butts, such as an umbrella stand filled with sand, outside the door. Chairs or a bench let smokers relax while they're waiting for laundry and enjoying a smoke. And a sign saying "Smoking Area" lets smokers know that they're still welcome at your laundry.

Snack Time

It's likely that your customers will get hungry and thirsty while they're waiting for their laundry to finish. Even if your store is near a shopping area, many customers wisely don't want to leave their clothes. So vending machines with sodas, chips and candy fit the bill. You can buy a vending machine, fill it yourself and take all the profits. Or you can contract with a vendor who will provide the machine and snacks and split the profits with you. Ask your distributor about vending companies in your area.

Clarkson and her partner decided to put in a snack counter rather than vending machines. They offer their customers—and anyone else who comes in—a soda in a glass with ice, along with candy bars and chips. The partners chose to go that route after talking with other laundry owners. "In interviewing other people, we found that [they] didn't like cans, they liked a fountain drink," Clarkson says.

They sell the snacks at a low cost because their store is next to a mini-mart. "If we had the same prices or higher, everyone would just go next door," Clarkson says. Still, their snack business is brisk enough that it brings in $30 to $60 a day. "Our Pepsi distributor says we do more [business] than some of his restaurants." Having the snack counter also improves customer relations, she says. "Our customers really appreciate the cheap prices."

The Attended
Laundry

As mentioned in the last chapter, many laundries offer their customers a variety of services to make their in-store experience more enjoyable. But besides offering amenities such as snacks or computers, there are other important services to consider for your start-up. If you plan to have an attended laundry, you should definitely consider offering laundry-related services, including wash-and-fold and an area to drop off and pick up dry cleaning. In this chapter, we'll explore how to incorporate these services into your store and profit from them.

We'll also look at what's involved in taking on employees to attend your store. We'll discuss some of the pros and cons of hiring attendants; then we'll get into the details of hiring, supervising and motivating employees.

Wash-and-Fold

According to Brian Wallace, president and CEO of the Coin Laundry Association, 65 percent of laundries offer wash-and-fold. If you're interested in starting this service (also called drop-off or fluff-and-fold), take a look at the neighborhood surrounding your laundromat. Customers who use wash-and-fold are usually middle- to upper-income types who may or may not have laundry equipment at home. They use the service primarily to save time. So if your laundry is located in an area that has residents with a range of income levels, wash-and-fold could be a good complement to your coin- or card-operated laundry business.

Some of our entrepreneurs have realized a tidy income from wash-and-fold, while others have not. Collette Clarkson, owner of The Last Load in Evans, Colorado, said that wash-and-fold brings in an extra $2,000 a month. "I don't know if we would be able to survive without it," she says.

But Cindy Patel, with Mountain Wash Laundry in Shelby, North Carolina, said wash-and-fold "isn't doing as well as we thought." But she continues to offer it because her laundry is attended, and it doesn't cost her any extra.

As long as you plan to have an attended laundry, there's little reason not to give wash-and-fold a try. Starting a wash-and-fold service will cost you little—possibly less than $500. Even if the service never quite becomes a hit, it can still bring in some money. You'll be paying your attendants the same amount whether they do wash-and-fold or not. In fact, many laundry owners offer their customers wash-and-fold service to help cover attendants' salaries.

Beware!

Clothing that is stained with grease, oil, or some other flammable substance could cause a dryer fire. Make sure anything you or your attendants wash is fully cleaned before it goes into a dryer. Also, watch for customers who throw clothing in the dryer without running it through the wash

How it Works

The equipment you'll need for a wash-and-fold service is minimal: a scale, a book of invoices, plastic laundry bags, stain removers, and detergent. You can buy a scale and the plastic bags

Beware! Many cleaning fluids contain solvents that are combustible and could burst into flames if they get too warm. So keep all cleaning fluids away from heat sources like washers, dryers, irons, heating elements, and water heaters.

from your distributor or a laundry supply company. You can purchase generic invoices from an office supply store, or you can have some printed up with your store's name and policies on them (see the sample invoice on page 82).

Once you start your wash-and-fold service, put up a sign in your laundry to let customers know you're offering this new service. Since they might not understand what "wash-and-fold" means, put up a sign that says something like, "We'll do your laundry for you." Also provide a counter so customers know where to bring their laundry. It helps to have a sign saying, "Drop your laundry here." In a large laundromat full of washers and dryers, folding tables, and vending machines, it's not always clear to customers where they should bring their clothes.

To provide basic wash-and-fold service, you or your attendant should follow these steps:

- *When customers bring in laundry for wash-and-fold, weigh it in front of them so they know how much it will cost.* Write the weight down on the invoice, along with the total cost. Make sure you get your customers' names and phone numbers in case they forget to pick up their clothes. Tell them when their clothes will be ready and give them their copy of the invoice.

    If the laundry is brought in damp or wet (customers sometimes bring in towels wet from the shower or swimming), note that on the invoice. This will help if customers are worried that some clothes are missing because the laundry weighs less when they pick it up than it did when they dropped it off.

- *Check the clothes for any stains and pre-treat them as well as you can.* There are several good books available for treating stains—see the Appendix for more information. These books can tell you what stain-removing products you'll need to buy and which of these products work best on different types of stains.

    Clarkson says she and her attendants do their best to remove all the stains on the clothes. "We don't charge extra," she says. But they also don't promise they'll be able to remove them. Check to make sure there's nothing in the pockets: Some items, such as lipstick tubes and pens, will stain the entire wash. Others, namely cigarette lighters, could explode in a dryer.

- *Wash and dry the laundry.* Follow the directions on clothing labels and make sure dark-colored items (especially those dyed red) are separate from the light-colored ones. Also be sure to keep each customer's laundry separate.

- *Fold the laundry.* Instruct your attendants to fold laundry the same way each time. Your repeat customers become accustomed to having their laundry folded

Laundry Invoice

Invoice No.: 5150

Sunbright Laundry
1000 Washtime Street
Clean Valley, TN 33333
(800) 555-1234

Today's date _____

Customer name _____

Customer phone _____

Order for pickup on:

S   M   T   W   TH   F   S   after _____ A.M./P.M.

Weight _____ Price _____ Total _____

Special instructions or conditions: _____

_____

_____

_____

_____

_____

_____

_____

_____

Not responsible for items left more than 30 days.

a certain way, and they section off their dresser drawers to fit the clothes.

- *Place the laundry in a plastic bag and weigh it again to make sure it weighs the same as it did when the customer brought it in.* This helps ensure that a few shirts or a pair of pants didn't end up in someone else's wash. When the customer comes to pick up the laundry, weigh it again to show him or her that it's all there.

Bright Idea

Asking customers to pay for wash-and-fold service ahead of time ensures that more of them will come back to pick up their laundry. A surprising number of customers never return for their clothes.

Pricing and Turnaround

The average charge for wash-and-fold service is between 80 and 90 cents a pound, with most laundry owners charging between 75 cents and $1.25. But in some cases, laundry owners will offer discounts or charge higher prices.

Tom Leavitt, who owns three Darcies Laundries in the Seattle area, for example, charges 20 cents less for large orders. On the other hand, many laundries charge extra for special instructions, such as cold water only for some items or delicate wash for selected items. You may also want to consider charging more for shirts that need to be placed on hangers or starched.

Wash-and-fold service is pretty speedy: Laundries often have clothes all washed and folded by the evening, provided that customers bring their orders in before noon. Some laundry owners give a one-day turnaround for clothes that require special instructions.

Left Behind

As strange as it may sound, some customers are going to leave their laundry with an attendant for wash-and-fold, then walk out the door and never come back. Some will also leave their laundry in the machines, then go run errands and never return.

Most states have a statute governing how long you have to hold onto unclaimed garments. It ranges from zero days to an indefinite amount of time, according to Brian Wallace of the Coin Laundry Association. "The best thing is to check with the attorney general or statutes in that state," he says. You can also search the web, using the keywords "unclaimed garment laws" and the name of your state.

Delivery

While offering wash-and-fold service provides your customers with the convenience they want, delivery takes that service to the next level. In response to customer demand for timesaving services, a few laundry owners are starting to make delivery part of the package. They pick up dirty laundry at customers' homes, take it to their stores, wash and fold it, and return it to the customer the next day.

This service works best for laundries that have a number of interested customers who live in close proximity to each other. "If [laundry owners] can get enough [interested customers] to establish some type of route, they are willing to take on a pickup and drop-off at an additional charge to the customer," says Paul Partyka, editor of *American Coin-Op* magazine. He notes that with so many two-income families, the need for this service is growing. A laundry can expect to earn about $1.25 per pound for delivery service.

Dry Cleaning

Many coin- or card-operated laundry owners also contract with a dry cleaner. They take clothes from customers and hold them for the dry cleaner—who later picks up the clothes, cleans them and brings them back. Clarkson says a dry cleaning service approached her and her partner about taking dry cleaning items. The partners get 30 percent of the profit on each order they take—just for tagging the clothes and storing them for the dry cleaner. Clarkson says it's a great deal: "We don't do much for that 30 percent."

If you have the room to store dry cleaning in your laundry, contact local dry cleaners and see if they are interested. These arrangements are usually beneficial to both you and the dry cleaner. You get a cut of their profits, and they get increased business because it's convenient for customers to bring all their clothes to one place.

Attending Your Laundry

As we mentioned earlier, not all laundry owners hire employees to attend their stores. Some decide they don't need the expense and don't want to spend the time supervising employees; others feel that having attendants makes their store more appealing to customers.

To Attend or Not to Attend

Probably the most important reason to hire attendants is to provide better customer service. When someone loses money in a machine, for example, an attendant can immediately issue a refund. Attendants make sure the soap machine is always stocked, the bathroom has toilet paper, and the floor is mopped up after a spill.

Leavitt and his partner didn't even consider running unattended laundries. They felt that to offer good customer service, someone would have to be in the store at all times.

Attendants who are friendly make customers feel welcome in your store. They can offer special amenities such as videos for the kids, free coffee, promotional discounts and wash-and-fold service. Attendants can also help customers use the machinery properly, which helps keep your equipment in good shape.

Patel said her attendants have been instrumental in introducing her customers to the card system. "If there's someone who's confused, we give them a tour around the store first," and walk them through the card system," she says. "In addition, they can steer customers toward the more profitable machines—front-load washers. Some customers avoid front-loaders because they are not sure how to use them."

Finally, attendants help prevent theft and vandalism. "That's why a lot of people do employ attendants," says Wallace. Attendants also make customers feel safer in your store, especially at night.

On the other hand, hiring employees adds a whole new dimension to your business. You have to find them, train them, supervise them, and most importantly, pay them. A few of the laundry owners interviewed for this book decided they wanted to simplify things and go unattended.

Brian De Coster, who owns Laundromania in Iowa City, Iowa, says he thought about hiring someone who could clean for him and do wash-and-fold service, but he decided against it. "I thought maybe I'd be able to make more with drop-off," he says, "but I didn't want the headache of hiring and supervising an employee." If you've decided otherwise and plan to hire someone to attend your laundry, read on.

Fitting the Description

If you'll be offering a wash-and-fold service, much of your attendants' time will be spent washing your customers' clothes. The job description should also include assisting customers with their laundry and the equipment. Attendants

▲

Team Uniform

Your customers can probably guess that the woman wiping down the machines is an employee at the store, but they might not know that the man doing wash-and-fold is an attendant—he looks like any other customer.

To help your customers know who to ask for help, you might want to give your attendants an identifying marker, such as a T-shirt with your laundry's name or logo. You could also supply your workers with aprons or buttons.

Collette Clarkson, owner of The Last Load in Evans, Colorado, says matching T-shirts are in the plans. In the meantime, she says, "Customers can figure out who's working there because they're serving sodas and constantly cleaning."

should watch for any customers who seem confused about how to work the machines or who appear to be looking for help. This is especially important if you have a card system. Most customers are used to a coin-operated laundry, but a card laundry might befuddle them enough to send them elsewhere.

Attendants should ease new customers into your store, said Paul Donovan, formerly of laundry equipment distributor PWS. If someone walks in and starts looking around, attendants should say, "'Hi, how are you? Let me show you how the soap works; give me your basket, and I'll run you through the process,'" he says. Part of an attendant's job is just to chat and be friendly with the customers. Once customers come to know and like the attendants in your store, they'll want to come back and see them.

Their main job, however, is to keep the laundry sparkling clean. "That's their job—to clean the laundromats," says Tim O'Connell, owner of Colonial Laundromats in the Syracuse area of New York. O'Connell's laundries are attended most of the time, but he doesn't offer wash-and-fold.

Attendants should clean as soon as there is any kind of mess or spill, rather than wait for closing time. Once the store closes and all the customers are gone, the attendants should thoroughly clean the entire store including the machines, the bathroom, and the floors. See Chapter 2 for more on the specific cleaning tasks that your attendants will need to take care of daily.

If you offer any amenities, such as videos or free lollipops for the children, your attendants will need to keep track of these supplies. And if you serve free coffee or snacks, your attendants will need to keep the coffeepot full and the snacks flowing.

You'll want to collect the money out of the machines and the changer yourself, but you'll have to let your employees take money for wash-and-fold and dry cleaning orders. Have your employees total the money in the cash register at the end of each day and put it in a safe place, along with the receipts. You can check the invoices against the cash drawer to make sure your employees aren't stealing from you.

Finally, your attendants need to keep track of your inventory of cleaning supplies, wash-and-fold materials, and vending items (if you own the machines). Figure out a system that attendants can use to let you know which supplies are getting low. A dry-erase board in the back room or even a notepad on the front counter can do the job.

Other duties for your attendants will include:

- Restocking vending machines (if you own the machines)
- Retrieving laundry carts from the parking lot
- Giving refunds on cards or for broken machines
- Marking broken machines so other customers will not use them
- Restocking bathroom supplies
- Emptying trash cans

Shifty Attendants

Most laundries have one attendant on duty at a time, though sometimes attendants' shifts will overlap a few hours during the busiest times of the day. Depending on the hours you are open and whether you want to hire full- or part-time employees, most likely there will be two to three shifts to cover per day, seven days a week.

If your laundry is open from 6 A.M. to 10 P.M. each day and an attendant spends an extra hour cleaning (until 11 P.M.), that means you have a total of 17 hours per day when you need someone to mind the store. There are a number of ways you could choose to cover these hours. If you only want to hire part-time employees, you could hire three attendants and have each work one six-hour shift per day, with the afternoon shift overlapping the evening shift to cover your busiest time of day.

The employee on the first shift would open the store at 6 A.M., help customers, and do the bulk of the wash-and-fold while business is slowest in the morning. The second-shift attendant would come in at noon and leave at 6 P.M., and would do wash-and-fold until business picks up in the late afternoon. At that point, he or she would then focus on customer service. The employee on the last shift, from 5 to 11 P.M., would assist customers, and he or

Tip...

Smart Tip

Show prospective hires the "Attendant Training Video" offered by the Coin Laundry Association (see the Appendix for contact information). The video will give them a good idea of the job duties they'll have to perform, and you can weed out those who aren't interested before you hire them.

she would do a thorough cleaning after the store closes. Don't forget that you'll need an additional employee to help cover weekend shifts, or you might choose to work some weekend shifts yourself.

Of course, some of your employees could work longer shifts and others shorter shifts. And some could work five days a week and others just a few days a week. The hours and days they work will likely depend on the hours you're open and your employees' availability. If you would prefer to have one or two full-time employees instead of several part-time employees your shift schedule will look a little different than the one we've just described. Also factor in the number of shifts that you will be able to work yourself. The more you can work, the more you will save on the cost of employee payroll and benefits.

> ## Smart Tip
>
> Tip...
>
> The more time you spend supervising your attendants—visiting the laundry, responding to their requests and checking on their performance—the less likely they are to steal from you or become frustrated with their job and quit. Don't just hire employees and split: Train them, talk with them, and evaluate their job duties regularly.

If you decide not to have an attended laundry, you might still want to hire someone to clean for you. You'll have to pay their salary, naturally, but since they'll be working only two to three hours per day, the cost to you won't be nearly as much as that of a full-time employee. For a part-time employee making a little above minimum wage, you're looking at about $500 per month as opposed to $1,500 per month in payroll and benefits for a full-time employee.

You may want to consider hiring retirees, as they're often interested in part-time work. Seniors also tend to be experienced and reliable. Dave and Kris Anderson clean their unattended New Glarus, Wisconsin, laundry themselves, but for a while they hired a retiree to clean part time. Clarkson says she uses a number of high school students, who are available during late afternoons and early evenings as well as weekends, the busiest time for laundries.

Hiring Hints

Most of the entrepreneurs interviewed for this book said that they found prospective attendants through their customers. These laundry owners advertised their available positions by putting up signs in their stores. Some of the attendants they hired were in fact customers, while others were friends and acquaintances of customers. "Oftentimes, it's a satisfied customer," Leavitt says. "That's a major way we find them. Oftentimes, they're referred by customers or other employees."

But O'Connell says that he avoided advertising in his laundry. "We don't put signs in the windows because the customers get mad if you don't hire them," he says. He advertises in newspapers: "If someone looks in the newspaper, they're really looking for a job; they're not just sitting there doing their laundry and thinking 'I'll take it.'"

When you're interviewing attendants, look for people you think will be good at handling customers. If you're considering hiring customers for wash-and-fold, watch how much care they take to do their laundry—if they don't handle their own clothes with care, they won't handle customers' well either.

And if many of your customers speak a language other than English, try to hire someone who speaks that language. A Spanish-speaking attendant will help draw those customers who are more comfortable speaking Spanish.

Training Time

The best way to train new employees is to have them work with either an experienced attendant or with you for several days. Walk them through the wash-and-fold procedure, working the cash machine, refilling the vending machines, cleaning the store and anything else that will be a routine part of the job.

Be sure to talk to new attendants about customer service and let them know what to do when a customer complains. Let your new attendants know what the policy is if a customer wants a free wash after a machine didn't spin out, for example. Also give

---

Employee Closing Tasks

It's a good idea to give your employees a checklist to make sure everything gets done before they close for the night. We've compiled a list of the basic tasks your employees will need to perform:

Cleaning
- ❏ Pick up trash off the floor, tables, and seats
- ❏ Sweep and mop the floor
- ❏ Clean dryer lint screens
- ❏ Wipe down all machines
- ❏ Wipe down folding tables
- ❏ Empty wastebaskets
- ❏ Clean restroom
- ❏ Gather carts and place them near washers
- ❏ Wash windows weekly
- ❏ Clean coffeepot

Front Counter
- ❏ Count cash in register
- ❏ Place cash and invoices in a safe place
- ❏ Mark and store forgotten clothes

Supplies
- ❏ Fill all vending machines
- ❏ Restock restroom supplies
- ❏ Check supply inventory
- ❏ Replace any burned-out bulbs

▲

your new attendants a checklist for closing down the store to make sure everything is cleaned, checked, and stocked on a daily basis. See page 89 for a checklist of employee closing tasks.

In addition, you might want to give your attendants some training in equipment maintenance. If your attendants know how to solve problems quickly, that means machines will be up and running—and earning money—more quickly. It also means you won't receive so many frantic phone calls. You can teach them what you know, or you can send them to equipment school—manufacturers offer training sessions for their equipment on a regular basis. Make sure you give your attendants your phone number when you're not at the store so they can reach you if they do have a problem they can't solve.

What's the Motive?

It's a challenge to inspire laundry attendants to do a great job. Attendants usually make little more than minimum wage—a recent Coin Laundry Association survey found that most laundry owners were paying their attendants between $5.50 and $7.50 an hour. There's also little room for advancement in a small company like a laundry, and there are often no benefits. But the laundry owners interviewed for this book said they gave as much financial incentive as they could afford to.

"We try to move them up a little quickly so we can pay a somewhat decent wage," says Clarkson. She adds, "We tried to do some really nice bonuses at Christmas time."

Leavitt gives the store managers, but not the attendants, a cut of the profits. "The only people who are part of an incentive pool are the managers," he explains. "We found it didn't have the full impact on the staff."

Laundry owners said they also tried to motivate their attendants by providing a fun work atmosphere. "We have fun, and we work right alongside them," Clarkson says.

It's to your advantage to keep employee turnover as low as possible. You won't waste valuable time and money training new attendants over and over again, and you will benefit from the experience that long-term employees gain after they have been on the job for a while. So how can you hang on to your employees? You'll have a head start if you treat them considerately, give them the training they need to do a good job, and offer them as much financial incentive as you can afford.

Promoting
Your Store

Now that your laundromat is ready for customers, it's time to do a little advertising. If your store is new, you'll need to introduce it to the community; if you've bought an existing one, you'll want to let customers know the store has a new owner. And if you've been operating for a while, you'll still want to do some advertising to bring in new customers—and hold on to your current ones.

In this chapter, we'll discuss the types of advertising that work for laundromats, including opening celebrations, Yellow Pages ads, in-store promotions, and mailers. We'll also cover what's probably the most effective form of advertising—customer service.

Of Advertising and Laundries

Laundry owners are not known for their sophisticated marketing techniques. In fact, says Brian Wallace, president and CEO of the Coin Laundry Association, "Most coin laundries do no advertising whatsoever." According to Wallace, most owners rely on business from customers who see their store when walking or driving past.

Laundry consultant Andrew Cunningham says that advertising helps promote wash-and-fold, but not the self-service business. "Laundries have glass ceilings," he says. "Once you've captured the market, it's highly unlikely you're going to increase business further." But he added that advertising can help build the market of a new store.

If you decide to promote your store, remember that a laundry draws its customers from its immediate neighborhood. You'll want to steer clear of radio, newspapers (unless it's a small weekly), and other media that reach the whole community because you'll spend a lot of money talking to people who will never use your laundry. Focus your marketing efforts on your immediate community: This includes people who live in the vicinity and those who shop or do business near your laundry.

Whatever form of promotion or advertising you decide to go with, make sure you can measure how well it works. If a promotion turns out to be a bomb, you'll want to avoid spending money on it in the future. *Start Your Own Business* by Rieva Lesonsky

Survey Says

Your customers are just sitting around your laundry week after week—why not put them to work for you? Each customer has valuable marketing information to offer, so take a survey.

You can ask your customers if a specific promotion, such as a "Singles Night," will help bring in business. You can ask if they would pay more for newer equipment, if they'd like to have free doughnuts on weekday mornings, or if making the switch to a card system would be worth the money.

Offer customers something in return for answering the survey, such as a reduced-price wash or a complementary box of soap. You'll get more responses, and you'll get less resentment from people who don't want to give away marketing information for nothing.

Dollar Stretcher

Have a set of business cards printed for your laundry—you can get 1,000 for as little as $15—and stamp on the back that they're good for a free wash. Distribute them everywhere: Leave them with waiters at restaurants, drop them in mail slots, and hand them to acquaintances.

(Entrepreneur Press, 2005) is a wonderful resource for ideas on developing your marketing plan, advertising your small business, and measuring the success of your advertising.

Grand Opening

Whether your store is new or you've recently purchased it, a grand opening celebration is a good way to let people know you are in business. Collette Clarkson, owner of The Last Load in Evans, Colorado, says sales jumped $1,000 in the week after she and her partner held their grand opening.

A grand opening usually involves a big advertising push for a day of opening celebrations at the laundromat. An enormous sign saying "Grand Opening" or a tent in the parking lot will draw in passersby. At the celebration, give prospective customers the chance to win prizes and snack on free food while they tour your recently built or renovated laundromat. If you want to throw a grand opening in a parking lot or on the sidewalk, check with your landlord and the city or county to see if you need a permit.

Brian De Coster, owner of Laundromania laundromats in Iowa City, Iowa, joined forces with neighboring businesses to help promote his laundry. He asked them to give away prizes, such as free coffee or haircuts, and in return he named them as co-sponsors in the advertising. He then took out a one-page ad in the local newspaper to call attention to the grand opening. On the day of the celebration, he put up a tent in the parking lot and gave away cotton candy and popcorn. He held a drawing every half an hour to give away the prizes from neighboring businesses, which included free movies, sandwiches and dry cleaning. "We gave away a couple thousand dollars in prizes," he says. "People loved it. It was real busy."

If many of your prospective customers will be families with children, try to include something in your grand opening that will appeal to kids, such as face painting, a drawing contest or free toys. Parents are always looking for cheap ways to entertain their offspring.

Run your new laundry for a few months before you have your grand opening to make sure you've ironed out any kinks. De Coster says he waited about a month before his grand opening. "We got a feel for the machines," he says, "[and] got the bugs worked out of [the store]."

Bright Idea

If you have a super-size washer, advertise it to the residents in the neighborhood where you have your store. Advertise even to those who wouldn't normally use a laundry. If you point out that it can wash large comforters, drapes, and even rugs, you might pull in some extra business.

If you have a card system, you can hand out wash cards to prospective customers with a small amount of money on them at your grand opening. Thrifty customers who want to take advantage of the savings will be encouraged to use the card at your store. When Cindy Patel held a grand opening for her Shelby, North Carolina, store, Mountain Wash Laundry, she handed out wash cards with $1 or $2 on them. Since then, she has continued to use the promotion: Because she also operates a motel, she gives them to her motel customers, and friends of hers who run a gas station hand them out to customers.

New Kid in Town

When you purchase an existing store—whether or not you renovate it—it's still a good idea to let customers know there's someone new at the helm. In all likelihood, the previous owner wasn't promoting the business or providing top-notch customer service. Why bother when he or she was planning on selling? If customers hear there's a new owner, they may be willing to give the store another try and see what the new owner has to offer.

You can simply put up a sign saying "New Owner" or "Under New Management." If you've added a coat of paint or made a few minor repairs, customers will already see the difference.

The Trusty Phone Book

Put yourself in the shoes of a potential customer: You've moved to an apartment in a new community. After a week, you notice that your socks are all dirty, your clothes are a mess from moving and the curtains in your apartment look like they've never been washed—you need to find a laundry fast. What do you do? Most likely, you're going to open the phone book and take a peek under "Laundry."

Laundromats are ideal for Yellow Pages advertising because people just need to find one that's conveniently located and open during the hours they need to do their laundry.

If you run an ad in the Yellow Pages, here are a few pointers:

- Make the phone number is bold or otherwise easy to see.
- Give directions or cross streets, not just the address.
- List the hours you're open.
- Make sure the type is uncluttered and easy to read.
- Use your logo if you have one.

De Coster saved some money in his Yellow Pages advertising by taking up just one line. He

Dollar Stretcher

If you have a computer, print out some fliers offering a reduced-price wash or dry. Place them on the windshields of cars in the parking lots near your store since people who run errands in the area are likely to use your laundry.

gives the name of his laundries and adds "24 hours," a big plus in his university town. His answering machine then states the location and repeats that it's open 24 hours per day.

Preaching to the Converted

A rule of thumb in advertising is that it's much cheaper to retain customers than find new ones. You can keep your customers coming back by offering a variety of discounts and in-store promotions.

Smart Tip

Tip...

Try offering free soap to your customers on certain days of the week or for special promotions. Buy detergent in bulk and hand it out in plastic cups—this is much cheaper than handing out individual boxes.

A common promotion is to offer customers a reduced-price wash during the day on Tuesdays, Wednesdays or Thursdays. These are the slowest times for most laundries, so it'll help you turn a profit just to have the machines in use. If you have a card system, you can program the machines to draw less money from the cards on those days.

If your machines take coins, you will need an attendant to give customers an extra coin. If a top-loader wash is normally $1.50 and you're offering it at $1.25, for example, your attendant can give customers a quarter. You can put up a sign saying, "Reduced-price wash! See attendant." Then have your attendant put the money in the machine for the customer—you don't want people coming in for free quarters.

You could also reward your loyal customers with a free wash after so many trips to your laundry. Use a punch card, or stamp the back of a business card. Some laundries reward their wash-and-fold customers by charging a lower price for dropping off bigger loads of laundry.

Lucky Logos

Think about developing a logo for your store. A logo, usually a simple picture or symbol, will come to represent your laundry and help you market it. Logos are often more recognizable than names.

You can use your logo in your store, on attendants' uniforms, on the signs outside, and on your delivery truck (if you have one). A logo is also a great advertisement to include on any marketing material, such as fliers, business cards, or coupons. Establish a standard of quality in your store, and customers will start associating your logo with quality. And if you want to expand, the logo will help customers easily recognize that you've opened an extension of the old store.

Some laundry owners try to draw in customers by offering free goodies in their stores, such as coffee or candy for kids.

Ideas that Worked—and Didn't

Every laundry and every neighborhood is different. What works like gangbusters for one laundry owner may fall flat for another, so it's difficult to generalize about the sort of marketing strategies that will work best for you. But here are a few tactics that worked for the entrepreneurs we interviewed:

- Tim O'Connell, owner of Colonial Laundromats in Syracuse, New York, advertises on cable TV and in the Penny Saver shopper. "It keeps our name out there," he says.
- Dave Anderson, who runs a laundry in the tourist town of New Glarus, Wisconsin, gets some vacationers' business by being included on a town map for tourists.
- Clarkson has had many customers respond to her "buy one wash/get one free" direct mailer.

On the flip side, here are some marketing tactics that didn't work at all:

- Tom Leavitt has a web site for his laundries, Darcies, but he doesn't believe it draws in any business.
- Clarkson tried advertising on the back of grocery coupons—with very little luck.

Word-of-Mouth

The best advertising is also the cheapest. If you have a nice, clean store with friendly attendants and working equipment, your customers are going to tell their friends and family members about it. In other words, the best way to promote your store is to offer great customer service. "Word-of-mouth works best," says Anderson. "If you keep it clean and people like the location, they'll tell people."

The laundry owners we spoke with said they try to provide top-quality customer service by keeping their laundries clean and in working condition at all times, by offering entertainment for adults and their children, and by being friendly and helpful. They also said it's important to be attentive to customers' needs. For example, Clarkson says that some of her customers have started visiting her laundry because other laundry owners kicked them out when the store closed—even though their washes had not finished. "You just don't do that," she says.

Clarkson adds, "Get to know your customers and let them feel like you really appreciate their business. Provide them with something to do. There's nothing more boring than sitting in a laundromat. Make it a fun place. A lot of our feedback has been that it's really fun to come here. It feels like home."

Once you have opened your business and started getting the word out to customers that yours is the best laundry in town, you'll need to get back to the books and see how well your business is coming along. In the next chapter, we'll look at accounting for laundromats—how to keep the books, price the services, and make sure you're turning a profit.

11

Counting
the Coins

We have already discussed how much you can expect to pay just to open a store, but what will it cost you to keep it running successfully? And what kind of profit can you expect to make from your store? In this chapter, we're going to show you how to keep track of the money you have coming in and going out each month. We'll look at what your monthly book-keeping will be like and how to approach pricing and filing taxes.

▲

Balancing the Books

Managing your finances is crucial because you must know how your business—every aspect of it—is doing. If you are on top of your income and expenses, you can discover whether you're offering your services at the right price. You can also assess whether your wash-and-fold service justifies the cost of a second employee or if you can afford to pay a janitor to do the cleaning. In addition, you can see how much you're spending on repairs to gauge when it's time to buy new equipment.

Ultimately, when you add up the numbers you can see if the laundry business is even working out for you—or if it's time to sell. You also need to track your income carefully so you have something to report at tax time. We'll get to this topic a little later in the chapter.

Incoming

One of the realities of owning a laundry business (especially if yours is a coin laundry) is that there are lots of bills and coins to count. Other entrepreneurs, like consultants for example, will usually earn a few large checks a month that they can just toss in the bank, holding on to the pay stubs for their records. As a laundry owner, however, you will need to count every coin and bill that comes into your store.

In Chapter 2, we drew up a chart that shows you how to keep track of the money each type of equipment or service brings in (see "Equipment Use Chart" on page 18). As we mentioned, this information will help you decide which machines and services are the most popular in your store, and it will also give you a complete daily or weekly income statement. Add any services you offer to the chart—wash-and-fold, dry-cleaning drop-off/pickup, and snack vending—and you will have an accurate picture of the money you are taking in.

While you may want to keep track of your income on a daily or weekly basis, since that's how you collect money, you'll also want to know what your income is on a monthly basis so you can determine your net income. Many of your expenses—utilities, rent, insurance—are charged by the month, so you will need to calculate your income and operating expenses monthly.

Using an accounting program like Microsoft Money or Intuit QuickBooks will save you time. The Coin Laundry Association also sells an accounting program designed specifically for laundry owners (see the Appendix). Each of these programs costs between $150 and $250. If you use a card system, remember that much of your income will be calculated for you automatically by the system software.

Let's walk through the ins and outs of determining your gross monthly income. This amount will depend on how much you charge for your machines and how many customers are using them. Most laundromats are charging close to $1.50 per wash for top-loaders. Front-loaders that can handle up to 18 pounds of laundry run about $1.75 per wash; 25-pounders cost about $2.50 per wash; 30-pounders cost about $3 per wash; and 35-pounders cost about $3.50 per wash. Dryers usually cost 25 cents for a predetermined amount of time, usually eight to 12 minutes.

Once you decide how much you'll be charging, you can easily figure out what your income will be if you know how many times each piece of equipment is used each day. You can't know that in advance, but according to *American Coin-Op* magazine, an average figure is about four times, or turns per day (TPD). If you multiply the amount you charge for each type of machine by four and add those numbers, you'll have a rough idea of how much you can expect to earn from self-service. You may be able to determine a more exact figure for turns per day by asking your distributor, a consultant or other laundry owners in your area.

For wash-and-fold service, laundry operators charge customers between 60 cents and $1 per pound. The amount of wash-and-fold work you can expect differs, depending on where you are located and how great the demand is for this convenience. If your laundry is located in a relatively wealthy area, you can expect more revenue from wash-and-fold work. Residents in lower-income areas aren't likely to be able to afford drop-off service to the same degree.

Finally, you have to take into account revenue from vending machines (snack and soda machines, as well as soap dispensers). The amount these machines bring in depends on how much business you do. A very small store will earn only $125 or so per year; a very large one as much as $4,000.

To calculate sample monthly income figures, we are going to revisit our two hypothetical laundry businesses: Suds-R-Us and Squeaky Clean. The sample income and operating expenses chart on page 103 shows the monthly revenue for the two businesses, with an itemized list of calculations per machine type or service. This figure is an estimate of the gross monthly income; you will not have the net income until monthly expenses have been deducted (we will get to this in the next section).

Suds-R-Us will have revenue from wash-and-fold service, dry-cleaning drop-off and pickup, vending machines, and washers and dryers. We will assume 100 pounds of wash-and-fold service per day, at 90 cents per pound. We've predicted a TPD (turns per day) of four for calculating the gross monthly income from washing machines and dryers. Top-loaders will cost $1.49 per wash, the 18-pound front-loaders $1.80 per wash, the 30-pound front-loaders $3 per wash, the 50-pound front-loaders $5 per wash, and the 75-pound front-loader $7 per wash. The dryers, costing 27 cents for 10 minutes, will run an average of 50 minutes each

Dollar Stretcher

You should encourage your customers to use front-load washers in your store, since these use less water and electricity.

load, for a total of $1.35 per load. To calculate revenue, we'll multiply the following:

Number of machines x TPD x Price per load x Days in a month (30)

The gross monthly income for Squeaky Clean is also shown in the chart on page 103. Since Squeaky Clean is an unattended laundry, the only revenue sources will be vending services and washers and dryers. We've also predicted a TPD of four for this business. Top-loaders will cost $1.50 per wash, the 30-pound front-loaders $3.25 per wash, and the 50-pound front-loader $5 per wash. The dryers, costing 25 cents for 10 minutes, will run an average of 50 minutes each

Dollar Stretcher

Ask your utility company if you can get a discount because you're a good customer. Suggest that you have some tempting offers from other companies, but that you'd like to keep using the current company. Often, utility companies will offer a small discount.

load, for a total of $1.25 per load. Again, we've multiplied the number of machines by the TPD by the price per load by the number of days in a month (which we've assumed to be 30).

Outgoing

Now that you've got an idea of what your income will look like, let's take a look at the kinds of monthly expenses you will encounter as the owner of a laundry business.

The average laundry owner pays $1 per month per square foot in rent, though this figure will vary widely based on where you are in the country. An urban setting in a high-rent area such as Manhattan or San Francisco is going to cost you as much as $2 per square foot per month, or $4,000 per month for an average-size 2,000-square-foot laundry. Lower-rent areas could be as little as $0.25 per square foot per month. The rent may or may not include the maintenance fees for landscaping, parking lot upkeep, snow removal, taxes, and so on.

Utilities—gas, water, sewer, and electric—are often the biggest expenses for laundromats. Let's say you have 40 washers and 40 dryers, which is probably typical for an average-to-large-size laundry. Depending on what your utility company charges, you are going to pay between $2,000 and $5,000 per month. It also depends on your equipment mix: The front-loaders are much more efficient than top-loaders, so the more front-loaders you have the more you'll save on utilities. This amount will also depend on how much use your machines get. The good news is that the more you're paying in utilities, the more you'll be making in revenue.

You'll also need insurance to cover you for damage (theft, fire, flood) and liability (slip-and-fall or other claims from customers). The cost of insurance is hard to generalize because it's based on so many factors: location, size of the laundry, whether it's attended, whether you have a security system, the hours you're open, how much coverage

Income and Operating Expenses

Income and operating expense calculations for Suds-R-Us are based on 10 top-load washers ($1.49 per wash), 10 18-pound front-loaders ($1.80 per wash), five 30-pound front-loaders ($3 per wash), five 50-pound front-loaders ($5 per wash), one 75-pound front-loader ($7 per wash) and 16 stacked dryers (32 individual dryers, at $1.35 per load). Suds-R-Us also has revenue from vending services. And since Suds-R-Us is attended, wash-and-fold service and dry-cleaning drop-off/pickup are also sources of revenue.

Squeaky Clean has 10 top-loaders ($1.50 per wash), four 30-pound front-loaders ($3.25 per wash), one 50-pound front-loader ($5 per wash), and 6 stacked dryers (12 dryers, costing $1.25 per load). Vending service is the only other source of revenue since this laundry is unattended.

Sources of Monthly Revenue	Suds-R-Us	Squeaky Clean
Top-loaders (# washers x 4 TPD x price x 30 days)	$1,788	$1,800
18-pound front-loaders (# washers x 4 TPD x price x 30 days)	2,160	
30-pound front-loaders (# washers x 4 TPD x price x 30 days)	1,800	1,560
50-pound front-loaders (# washers x 4 TPD x price x 30 days)	3,000	600
75-pound front-loader (# washers x 4 TPD x price x 30 days)	840	
Dryers (# dryers x 4 TPD x price x 30 days)	5,184	1,800
Vending	1,400	540
Wash-and-fold (100 lbs. x $0.90 x 30 days)	2,700	0
Dry-cleaning drop-off/pickup	500	0
Gross Monthly Income	**$19,372**	**$6,300**
Monthly Expenses		
Rent	$3,000	$1,500
Utilities	3,700	1,850
Insurance	400	100
Advertising/promotions	150	0
Payroll (with taxes and overtime)	4,000	0
Repairs	0	350
Loan payment	1,500	500
Miscellaneous expenses	750	250
Total Monthly Expenses	**$13,500**	**$4,550**
NET MONTHLY INCOME	**$5,872**	**$1,750**

▲

you want, and whether you want business interruption coverage. Insurance costs can range between $100 and $400 per month for a policy that covers damage and liability.

Paying your employees and providing benefits will be another big cost. Laundry attendants earn wages that are slightly above the minimum wage, somewhere around $6 to $10 per hour. Let's say you pay $6.75 per hour and your employees work a collective total of 420 hours per month. That means your payroll will be $2,835 per month, just for hourly wages. You'll have to pay more—about $1,500 a month—for workers' compensation, Social Security and benefits, should you choose to offer them.

It's easy to remember the biggies—utilities, rent, salaries—but those little expenses add up, too. Miscellaneous expenses—soap, cleaning supplies, invoices for wash-and-fold, toilet paper, etc.—will cost you between $200 and $1,000 per month. Equipment repairs will depend on how old your machines are. If they're new, they won't be needing repairs. But if they're 5 years old, you can expect to pay about $1,000 per month for parts and labor for a store with 40 machines.

Take another look at the income and operating expenses chart on page 103 to view the operating costs incurred by our two hypothetical laundry businesses. To calculate the monthly expenses for Suds-R-Us, we have assumed that the owner pays his three employees $6.75 per hour, and that $1 per square foot per month is the going rate for rent (for the 3,000-square-foot store). Since Suds-R-Us is newly constructed, we've also taken into account that the equipment is new, still under warranty, and requires no upkeep.

Squeaky Clean, on the other hand, employs no attendants, and the rental cost is $1.50 per square foot per month (for a 1,000-square-foot space). Since the owner bought an existing laundry, we're also assuming that the equipment is 5 years old and that the warranty has expired (so there are monthly repair costs to cover, too). The owner did buy three new machines, which are covered under a parts and service warranty.

To arrive at a figure for net monthly income, simply subtract monthly operating expenses from gross monthly income. The net monthly incomes for our two hypothetical laundries are found at the bottom of the income and operating expenses chart.

The Bottom Line

As we mentioned, you'll need to know your income and expenses in excruciating detail for tax purposes. If, heaven forbid, the IRS decides to audit you, you must be able to substantiate your expenses.

You'll be able to figure out your own projected net income once you find a potential location for your laundromat (see Chapter 3) and have chosen a distributor (see Chapter 6). With these basics in place, you'll have a much better idea of what your projected monthly expenses will be like. In addition, you'll be able to determine your rent, utility rates, and any sewer connection fees that you may have to pay.

The distributor can tell you how many and what types of machines you'll want to install, and the equipment manufacturer can tell you how much gas, electricity, and water the equipment will use. Once you have a location, you can also get an estimate on insurance. Add employees' salaries (if you'll be hiring any), miscellaneous expenses, and the monthly payments on your loan, and you'll have your monthly costs.

The big question, of course, is how much you'll make. To be on the safe side when you calculate your projected monthly income, you may want to assume that your equipment does only three turns per day. Make another conservative estimate for what you'll make from wash-and-fold, dry cleaning, and vending income each month. Add these figures and subtract your expenses from your income—then you will have your projected net monthly income. Before you sign a lease, and before you buy any equipment, make sure that the net is something you can live with.

The Price Is Right

Setting a price for your equipment and services can be a little tricky. You can charge only as much as customers are willing to pay. And you have to consider the fact that if you raise prices, some of your customers may visit your competitor down the street.

Laundry owner Cindy Patel in Shelby, North Carolina, charges 69 cents a wash for her top-loaders. She says she hasn't been able to make a profit, but when she raised her prices, her customers went elsewhere. "I didn't think people would think about a 25-cent difference," she says, "but they do." Her competitors charge 50 or 75 cents a wash.

Yet laundry experts caution against worrying too much about the competition. If you charge so little you're losing money, you might as well close up shop. Charging impossibly low prices just keeps the whole industry down, adds Paul Partyka of *American Coin-Op* magazine.

Besides, a store that charges a higher price has more money to spend on the amenities and services that bring customers back, like working TVs, functioning equipment, and clean floors.

Bright Idea

Price your front-load washers so they offer a better value than top-loaders. Twenty-five-pound front-loaders can hold three loads, for example, so price them less than three times the cost of using top-loaders. If you charge $1.50 per wash for a top-loader, charge $3 per wash for a 25-pounder.

Brian De Coster, who runs four laundries in Iowa City, Iowa, says that he was nervous when he raised his top-loader prices from $1.25 to $1.50 per wash. It made his laundry the most expensive in the area, but the customers continued to come back. He feels that the extra amenities he offers justified the price increase. "I'm offering good quality equipment, good quality water [because of a water softener that he installed], and good drying," he says.

Andrew Cunningham, a former laundry owner and a laundry consultant, offers one tactic to avoid intense competition: If everyone else is charging 75 cents per wash for a top-load washer and that price is too low for you to make a profit, put in all front-loaders. "Avoid the argument altogether," he says. This may not work for your laundry, but you could emphasize your front-loaders rather than top-loaders.

Finally, if you raise your prices, you might find that your competitors follow suit. De Coster found that to be the case when he raised his prices.

Whether you have a card system or coin-operated machines, you can change prices relatively easily. For a card system and newer coin machines, you program in a new price. For older machines with slide systems, you change the number of slots that are open in the slide. Slide machines typically have eight quarter-slots—if you charge $1 a wash, you open four of the slots. To increase the price, you open up one more slot. Then, if you find you're losing too many customers, you can always switch back.

Tax Time

April 15th is the one time of the year you'll have a leg up on consultants and other low-overhead entrepreneurs. You will have lots and lots of deductions. Everything you buy for your laundry, from washing machines to paint for the restroom, is a deduction. Rent, utilities, paychecks, and insurance are obvious, but don't forget all those little deductions, including the paper you buy for fliers you distribute in the parking lot, association dues, even flowers you bring to your store to freshen it up.

Here are a number of tax deductions that, as a laundry owner, you should not overlook:

- *A home office.* If you use some part of your home for your administrative tasks, you may qualify for a deduction. However, it must be a space solely dedicated to your business.
- *Mileage between laundries.* This may apply if you own more than one store; however, you may not deduct the miles from home to your laundry. You can deduct mileage when you travel to buy supplies or parts.
- *Clothing left behind.* If you donate the clothing that customers leave in your store, you may be able to deduct the value of the clothes on your tax return (check your state's laws). When you donate the items to charity, ask for a receipt for tax purposes.

- *City licenses or fees.* The sewer connection fees you'll have to pay when you open your laundry are tax deductible, in addition to any other business licenses you have to pay for.
- *Refunds.* The money that you refund to customers who lost (or claimed they lost) money in your machines is also deductible—as long as you weren't able to recover the money in a machine.
- *Counterfeits.* You may be able to deduct any slugs or counterfeit bills that end up in your machines. Hold onto these in case you are audited.
- *Office equipment.* You can deduct the computer equipment you buy for accounting purposes.
- *Phone calls.* These are deductible if you make business-related calls from home.
- *Business-related publications.* You may also deduct the cost of subscriptions for any industry-related magazines and newsletters.

Your major equipment—washers, dryers, and water heating systems—may be depreciated over five years. This lets you spread out the expense and the deductions over that time. Alternatively, in some circumstances you may be able to deduct as much as $102,000 of your equipment expenses in one year, rather than depreciate it over five years. You may find that this is advantageous, depending on your tax bracket.

Sales Taxes Too?

Some states charge coin laundries sales taxes on their services. As of 2005, these states include Washington, New Mexico, Iowa, Hawaii, Louisiana, and West Virginia. Wisconsin charges tax on card-operated laundries only, since its laws state that coin-operated laundries are exempt.

The national Coin Laundry Association, its affiliates, and other regional associations are fighting the sales tax. They are arguing that laundries provide a basic health service, such as food and medicine, so they should not be taxed; most customers of self-service laundries have lower income, so they can't afford the tax; and coin laundry owners already pay taxes on their equipment when they purchase it.

Laundry associations have hired lobbyists and have had some success in changing these laws so that self-service laundries are excluded. If you're in one of the states affected by the sales tax and you want to help fight it, contact your local coin laundry association.

Beware!
Don't throw away your receipts once you've filed your tax returns. For equipment that you depreciate, you want to hold onto the receipts for at least as long as the depreciation—likely five years. Five years after that is even better, since the IRS may still ask for your receipts.

Laundry owners may also qualify for some tax credits. These are even better than deductions because the money you spend is subtracted from your total tax bill. Renovating your laundry to comply with the Americans with Disabilities Act can give you a tax credit, though only up to $5,000.

Hiring disadvantaged employees—such as a recipient of Aid to Families with Dependent Children, an ex-felon, a high-risk youth, a veteran, or someone in vocational rehabilitation—may qualify you for a tax credit. But CPA Richard Weisinger cautions that reliable employees are worth much more than tax credits, so be as careful as you normally would in hiring these employees.

Check with an accountant or tax specialist to verify that you are qualified for the tax deductions and credits you plan to claim. Tax laws can change, and your accountant should be able to tell you what is a legitimate deduction and what isn't.

Staying
on Top

Now that we've covered the basics of start-

ing a laundry business and running the day-to-day and month-

to-month operations, it's time to turn to some troubleshooting.

In this closing chapter, we'll discuss several of the potential

problems that you should prepare for as the owner of a laun-

dry, including vandalism, theft and lawsuits. We'll also

▲

offer some ideas on how to reduce utility costs and maximize your income. In short, we'll look at the factors that will enhance your success in the laundry business.

Smart Tip

Keep your video surveillance camera tapes as long as possible: Customers who claim they've been injured in your store have up to a year to file a personal injury lawsuit.

Vandals and Thieves

Vandalism and theft frequently pose problems for owners of unattended laundries, particularly when those laundries are located in rough neighborhoods. The laundry owners interviewed for this book say they've had vandals do a variety of damage to their stores: torching change machines, damaging washers and dryers, throwing a laundry cart through a plate-glass window, and stealing a TV remote control.

Occasionally, a clever thief will get hold of a key for the coin boxes on washers and dryers or for the bill changer and start removing the cash. According to the Coin Laundry News, one laundry owner realized someone had been skimming coins from the machines after a customer mentioned how nice his "employee" was. The thief had the foresight to take only a little bit each time to avoid being discovered.

Many laundry owners avoid the theft and vandalism problem by hiring attendants. Other laundry owners use security cameras and let their customers know they're being watched. Brian De Coster of Iowa City, Iowa, put a positive spin on the security cameras placed around his store. He wanted to let customers know they were being taped, but rather than saying, "Watch yourself—we're taping you," his signs say, "Security cameras for your protection." De Coster says, "It's keeping people pretty much on the straight and narrow."

By collecting money frequently and varying the time you pull coins from your machines, you can help to avoid theft (as discussed in Chapter 2). You'll also know that someone is stealing if you find that the number of coins in your coin boxes doesn't add up—if you charge $1 a wash, for example, and the coins total $3.75.

Beware!

Read your water meter on a daily or weekly basis to find out what's normal for your store. Also compare the water usage against your income. If the water meter stays the same but income drops, there may be a leak somewhere, or someone may be stealing from you.

Staying Out of Court

Another reason to hire attendants or add security cameras is to avoid "slip-and-fall" lawsuits or other personal injury claims. Someone who tries to make a bogus claim won't get very far if attendants are on hand or if video cameras are hooked up to record the nonincident.

Brian Wallace, president and CEO of the Coin Laundry Association says that while laundries are no more prone to these types of lawsuits than other stores, the lawsuits do occur. He adds that 90 percent of claims against laundries are of the slip-and-fall variety, and that a high percentage of those are fraudulent.

If you or an attendant sees a customer fall or become injured in your store, make a careful record of what happened and what conditions in the store led to the accident (if any). If you have security cameras in your store, keep the videotape.

Should a lawyer contact you regarding a claim, contact your insurance agent immediately. He or she can advise you on how to handle the situation. It's generally best not to give the lawyer any additional information until you have spoken with your insurance agent personally.

Risk Prevention Checklist

To help protect yourself against lawsuits, you'll need to guard against hazards. Use this checklist to identify some of the potential risks to your customers. There may be additional hazards unique to your store, so you should discuss safety issues with your distributor or consultant.

Outside the store
❑ Repair or mark any cracks or holes in the sidewalk outside your store.

❑ Mark plate-glass windows so customers won't walk through them.

❑ Clearly mark any steps into your store and inside the laundromat.

Inside the store
❑ Install slip-proof flooring.

❑ Make sure the floor is clear of debris.

❑ Immediately fix any broken tiles or holes in the floor.

❑ Buy cones or signs that say "Wet floor," and use them when cleaning.

❑ Use bright lighting, but be sure it doesn't cause glare.

❑ Be sure your equipment is working properly.

❑ Clearly mark broken machines.

❑ Cover or repair any rough or sharp edges on equipment.

❑ Lock any closets or back rooms containing cleaning equipment and solutions.

❑ Teach your attendants how to respond in an emergency.

❑ Install enough fire extinguishers.

❑ Clearly mark an emergency exit.

The best way to avoid lawsuits is to make sure your store is a safe place to do laundry. The fact that someone was hurt in your store doesn't necessarily make you liable—you're liable only if you neglect to create a safe environment. If you have a store that has loose tiles that customers can trip over and pools of water that can cause customers to slip, you're going to have a harder time fighting a lawsuit successfully. Says Wallace, "You need to keep the store well-maintained and in good working condition."

Cutting Costs

When you are looking for ways to increase your income, don't just look at growing your customer base. While a big group of happy customers will keep you running to the bank, you can also increase your net profit by reducing costs.

Your laundromat has fixed expenses that you can't change, such as rent and insurance. But it also has variable expenses that can change such as salaries, supplies, and utilities. It's worth taking a look at your variable expenses to see if there's a way to increase your profits.

The area with possibly the greatest potential for reducing costs is utilities—one of the larger, if not the largest, expense you'll have. If you take a look around your laundry, you may find several ways to reduce your utility bills. Here are some ideas to get you started:

Drought Days

Many parts of the country face water restrictions when a drought occurs. If customers have water restrictions to comply with, laundromats will feel the effect. The good news is that business often increases during a drought. Many people who have their own laundry equipment will use self-service laundries to reduce their home water use. They'll save the water to keep their lawns alive and to enjoy long showers. Apartment complexes may also close their laundry facilities in order to reach water reduction requirements.

The bad news is that local water boards may penalize laundromats for using more water, despite the fact that doing so would be counterproductive. Equipment in laundromats is usually more water efficient than home or apartment machinery.

If your area has been suffering through a drought and water restrictions are going to be implemented, link up with other laundry owners and try to approach your water board before it votes to issue penalties. Also enlist help from your local coin laundry association.

- *Try lowering the temperature of your water heater.* Most laundry owners keep their water at about 140° Fahrenheit, but you may find your customers are just as happy with a lower temperature.

- *Make sure your dryer vents are clean.* Clogged vents lower the efficiency of dryers, causing them to use more energy. A chimney sweep can clean the vents for you.

- *Look at the flame on your gas dryers.* If the flame is yellow and flickering, gas is being wasted; the flame should be bright blue and should rise straight up. Contact your gas company to adjust the flame—many will do this free of charge.

- *Insulate your water tank.* If your tank wasn't insulated when you purchased or built your laundromat, have your contractor do it now.

- *Inspect your water lines.* Make sure that you don't have a leak somewhere and that your meter isn't attached to a neighbor's system. Otherwise, you could be paying for the water of the restaurant next door.

- *Put your lights on timers.* You can turn off those lights that are right next to windows during daylight hours. At night, when the laundry is closed, keep on only those lights you need for security, such as the ones above the change machine and near the door.

- *Consider the efficiency of your machines.* If you have older washers that use more energy and water than newer ones, replacing them may save you money in the long run.

Keys to Success

The key to a successful laundromat can be summed up in two words: customer service. Provide an atmosphere that customers appreciate, make customers and employees feel appreciated, and keep equipment in good working condition. Although the competition in some areas is tight, if you offer good customer service, you can often win over customers from other less inspired laundromats. If your laundry has an atmosphere that's more fun, and your attendants are friendly, your customers will keep returning because they'll feel more comfortable there.

In our interviews with laundry owners and experts for this book, one other point became clear to us. Laundry owners who spend time in their stores getting to know customers and who supervise their attendants closely reap the most from the business—both financially and personally. Owners who visit their stores only to collect money and wipe down a few machines make less money and tend to dislike the business more than owners who have a greater sense of commitment.

In short, the more you put into your business, the more you will get out of it. With commitment, your laundry will be a business that not only creates a tidy profit for you but that also gives you a sense of enjoyment and the satisfaction of a job well-done. So what are you waiting for? Take what you've learned in these pages and get started on your new venture as a laundry professional!

Appendix
Home Inspection Resources

They say you can never be rich enough or young enough. While these could be argued, we believe you can never have enough resources. Therefore, we're giving you a wealth of sources to check into, check out, and harness for your own personal information blitz.

These sources are tidbits—ideas to get you started on your research. They are by no means the only sources out there, and they should not be taken as the ultimate answer. We have done our research, but businesses do tend to move, change, fold, and expand. As we have repeatedly stressed, do your homework. Get out there and start investigating!

As an additional tidbit to get you going, we strongly suggest the following: If you haven't yet joined the internet age, do it! Surfing the net is like waltzing through a library, with a breathtaking array of resources literally at your fingertips.

Associations

Coin Laundry Association, 1315 Butterfield Rd., #212, Downers Grove, IL 60515, (630) 963-5547, www.coinlaundry.org

International Fabricare Institute, (organization for dry cleaners, wet cleaners and launderers), 14700 Sweitzer Ln., Laurel, MD 20707, (800) 638-2627, www.ifi.org

Books

Business Plans Made Easy, 3rd edition, David H. Bangs, Jr., Entrepreneur Press, www.entrepreneurpress.com

Don Aslett's Stain-Buster's Bible: The Complete Guide to Spot Removal, Don Aslett, Penguin USA

Financing Your New or Growing Business: How to Find and Raise Capital for Your Venture, Ralph Alterowitz and Jon Zonderman, Entrepreneur Press, www.entrepreneurpress.com

How to Buy and Sell a Business, Garret Sutton, Warner Business Books

How to Clean Practically Anything, The Editors of Consumer Reports, Consumer Reports Books

How to Get a Small Business Loan: A Banker Shows You Exactly What to Do to Get a Loan, Bryan E. Milling, Sourcebooks Trade

Start Your Own Business: The Only Start-Up Book You'll Ever Need, 3rd edition. Rieva Lesonsky, Entrepreneur Press, www.entrepreneurpress.com

The Queen of Clean: The Royal Guide to Spot and Stain Removal, Linda Cobb, Pocket Books

The 10-Minute Marketer's Secret Formula: A Shortcut to Extraordinary Profits Using Neighborhood Marketing, Tom Feltenstein, Entrepreneur Press, www.entrepreneurpress.com

Ultimate Small Business Advisor: All You Need to Know, Andi Axman, Entrepreneur Press, www.entrepreneurpress.com

Consultants

Lionel Bogut, P.O. Box 2175, Sun City, CA 92586, (951) 301-7644

Andrew Cunningham, Cunningham Consultants, 3812 Sepulveda Blvd., Torrance, CA 90505, (310) 951-4556

Richard Weisinger, CPA, 440 Western Ave., #201, Glendale, CA 91202, (818) 546-1094

Demographics Services

Claritas, 5375 Mira Sorrento Pl., #400, San Diego, CA 92121, (800) 866-6520, www.claritas.com

GeoVue, 500 W. Cummings Park, # 2050, Woburn, MA 01801, (888) 554-5150, www.geovue.com

Distributors

Coin Laundry Association, (includes a list of distributors by state), www.coinlaundry.org

Bob Eisenberg, Qualclean Equipment, P.O. Box 1505, Blue Bell, PA 19422, (800) 281-6878, e-mail: bob@qualclean.com

Educational/Training Videos

"Building a Coin Laundry from the Ground Up" Coin Laundry Association, 1315 Butterfield Rd., #212, Downers Grove, IL 60515, (630) 963-5547, www.coinlaundry.org

"Coin Laundry Association, Attendant Training Video" Coin Laundry Association, 1315 Butterfield Rd., #212, Downers Grove, IL 60515, (630) 963-5547, www.coinlaundry.org

"Choosing the Right Location for Your Laundry" Coin Laundry Association, 1315 Butterfield Rd., #212, Downers Grove, IL 60515, (630) 963-5547, www.coinlaundry.org

"Coin Laundry Employees: How to Find, Hire and Train" Coin Laundry Association, 1315 Butterfield Rd., #212, Downers Grove, IL 60515, (630) 963-5547, www.coinlaundry.org

"How to Buy a Coin Laundry" California Coin Laundry Association, P.O. Box 39277, Downey, CA 90239, (562) 861-6106, www.coinlaundromat.com

"How to Operate a Coin Laundry" California Coin Laundry Association, P.O. Box 39277, Downey, CA 90239, (562) 861-6106, www.coinlaundromat.com

Equipment Vendors

American Changer Corp., (sells coin changers), 1400 NW 65th Pl., Fort Lauderdale, FL 33309, (959) 917-3009

Brighton Parts and Supply (sells machine parts and laundry, equipment), 2384 Coney Island Ave., Brooklyn, NY 11223, (800) 727-8754, e-mail: brightonparts@hotmail.com

Card Concepts Inc. (sells card systems), 302 S. Stewart Ave., Addison, IL 60101, (866) 860-1660, www.laundrycard.com

Carolina Vending Equipment (sells vending machines), 700 E. Standing Springs Rd., Simpsonville, SC 29680, (800) 348-6543, www.carolinavendingequip.com

Coin-Op Sales Corp., 201 N. Howard St., #400, Dallas, TX 75201, (800) 434-7658

Partsking.com (an online store for machine parts), (800) 462-4814, www.partsking.com

R&B Wire Products (sells laundry carts), 2902 W. Garry St., Santa Ana, CA 92704, (800) 634-0555, www.rbwire.com

Vend-Rite (sells vending machine products, soap, and hanger vending machines, laundry bags, and signs), 2555 W. Armitage, Chicago, IL 60647, (800) 777-1802

Magazines and Newsletters

American Coin-Op, 500 N. Dearborn St., Chicago, IL 60610-4901, (312) 337-7700

The Journal, 1315 Butterfield Rd., #212, Downers Grove, IL 60515, (630) 963-5547, e-mail: journal@coinlaundry.org

Coin Laundry News, 26836 Cherry Hills Blvd., Sun City, CA 92586, (909) 301-7644, e-mail: clnews@inland.net

Manuals

California Coin Laundry Association Owner's Manual, P.O. Box 39277, Downey, CA 90239, (562) 861-6106, www.coinlaundromat.com

California Coin Laundry Association Reference Manual, P.O. Box 39277, Downey, CA 90239, (562) 861-6106, www.coinlaundromat.com

Successful Coin Laundry Owners

Alpine Laundry, Dave and Kris Anderson, 16 14th Ave., New Glarus, WI 53574, (608) 527-2690

Colonial Laundromats, Tim O'Connell, P.O. Box 346, Nedro, NY 13120, (315) 469-5593

The Last Load, Collette Clarkson and Kim Clarkson, 3230 23rd Ave., #100, Evans, CO 80620, (970) 339-9210

Laundromania, Brian De Coster, 737 Mormontrek, Iowa City, IA 52246, (319) 337-7368

Mountain Wash Laundry, Cindy Patel, 825 W. Dixon Blvd., Shelby, NC 28152, (704) 482-3821

Web Sites

Coin Laundry Association bulletin board, www.coinlaundry.org

Coinwash.com, (a bulletin board for laundry owners and marketplace of laundries for sale), www.coinwash.com

Glossary

Card system: a payment method that involves using prepaid swipe cards (much like phone cards) instead of coins.

Distributor: someone who sells laundry equipment and works for a specific manufacturer in a certain geographic area.

Drop-off: see wash-and-fold.

Extractor: a machine that extracts water from laundry by spinning it at a high speed.

Fabricare: the business of taking care of fabric, whether it be wash-and-fold, dry cleaning, or wet cleaning.

Fluff-and-fold: see wash-and-fold.

Front-load washer: a large-capacity washing machine that can clean from 18 to 80 pounds of laundry at once; a washer with a door on the front and a drum inside.

Impact fees: also called sewer connection fees or washer hook-up fees; the fees a municipality or water district will charge a laundry business for connecting washers to sewer lines.

Pro forma: an analysis of the expected income and expenses from a laundry business that's for sale.

Pull: collecting coins from machines.

Route operator: someone who services laundry machines in residential buildings such as apartments, condominiums, and dormitories.

Sewer connection fees: see impact fees.

Stacked dryer: a piece of equipment that contains two dryers placed on top of the other in a joined cabinet casing.

Top-load washer: the standard washing machine you find in homes; this type of washer has a door on the top of the machine and an agitator in the middle.

TPD: turns per day; see also turn.

Tumbler: the horizontal drum inside a dryer or front-load washer.

Turn: the number of times a machine is used each day.

Wash-and-fold: a service that allows customers to drop off their laundry and have it washed and folded for them; also called drop-off and fluff-and-fold.

Washer hook-up fees: see impact fees.

Wet cleaning: an alternative to dry cleaning that uses water rather than solvents to remove dirt and stains from clothing.

Index